HOW THEY CROAKED

First published in the United States of America in March 2011 by
Walker Books for Young Readers, an imprint of Bloomsbury Publishing, Inc.
Paperback edition published in July 2012
www.bloomsbury.com

Bloomsbury is a registered trademark of Bloomsbury Publishing Plc

For information about permission to reproduce selections from this book, write to
Permissions, Bloomsbury Children's Books, 1385 Broadway, New York, New York 10018
Bloomsbury books may be purchased for business or promotional use. For information on bulk purchases
please contact Macmillan Corporate and Premium Sales Department at specialmarkets@macmillan.com

The Library of Congress has cataloged the hardcover edition as follows:
Bragg, Georgia.
How they croaked : the awful ends of the awfully famous / by Georgia Bragg ;
illustrated by Kevin O'Malley. —1st U.S. ed.
p.   cm.
ISBN 978-0-8027-9817-6 (hardcover) • ISBN 978-0-8027-9818-3 (reinforced)
1. Celebrities—Death—Juvenile literature. 2. Death—History—Juvenile literature.
3. Biography—Juvenile literature. I. O'Malley, Kevin, ill. II. Title.
CT105.B725 2011   920—dc22   2010008659

ISBN 978-0-8027-2794-7 (paperback)

Art created with Black Micron 005 by Pigma on layout paper
Typeset in Centaur
Printed in China by C&C Offset Printing Co., Ltd., Shenzhen, Guangdong
11 13 15 17 19 20 18 16 14 12 10 (hardcover)
3 5 7 9 10 8 6 4 (reinforced)
9 10 (paperback)

All papers used by Bloomsbury Publishing, Inc., are natural, recyclable products made from wood grown in well-
managed forests. The manufacturing processes conform to the environmental regulations of the country of origin.

HOW THEY CROAKED

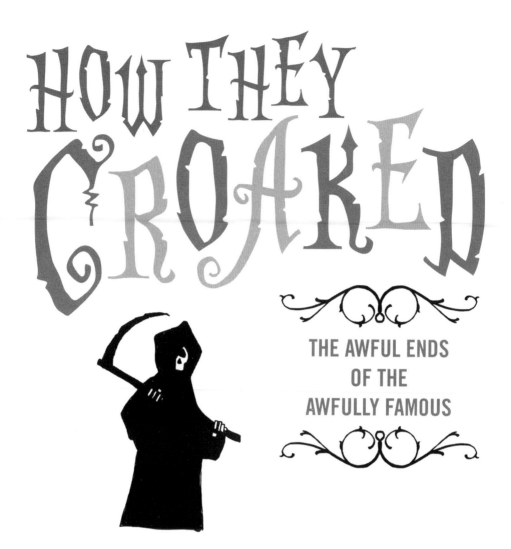

THE AWFUL ENDS OF THE AWFULLY FAMOUS

GEORGIA BRAGG

ILLUSTRATED BY KEVIN O'MALLEY

BLOOMSBURY

NEW YORK LONDON OXFORD NEW DELHI SYDNEY

CONTENTS

INTRODUCTION

WARNING:
If You Don't Have the Guts for Gore,
Do Not Read This Book

REMEMBER WHEN YOU watched *Bambi* for the first time and you got to the part where Bambi's mom dies? And the sweet movie about a family of deer turns into a horror flick? "What the heck was that?" you thought. And in that second you realized that if Bambi's mom can die, so can everybody else.

How They Croaked is like reliving Bambi's mom's death over and over again. Except it's worse because it's the blood, sweat, and guts of real people. In this book are the true stories of how some of the most important people who ever lived—died.

You probably don't know how George Washington, Cleopatra, or Beethoven ate it because every other book you've read skipped over that part. The reason is: getting sick and dying can be a big, ugly mess and, mostly, it's just sad.

There are nice things to say about everybody, but this book is full of bad news. There are funny crying parts and disgusting stupid parts and hideous cool parts, but it's pretty much one train wreck after another. And who can tear their eyes away from a train wreck?

Whether someone had a lung explode or was stabbed to death, died of poison or of a sore throat, there's always someone to blame, fingers to point. Looking back from where we sit now, people a long time ago sure did some dumb stuff—and it's definitely the kind of stuff worth writing about.

Even though everybody in this book has been dead a long time, reading about their last dying days will make your toes curl. But these stories will also fascinate you and make you realize how lucky you are to live in a world with painkillers and X-rays and soap and 911.

Who knows, maybe people in the future will look back at us and wonder, what the heck were *they* thinking? So here's a warning: take care of yourself, the world, and everybody in it. But if you don't have the guts for gore, DO NOT READ THIS BOOK.

KING TUT

BACK UP
THE U-HAUL

King of Egypt
Born: Egypt,
circa 1342 BC
Died: Egypt,
1323 BC
19 years old

KING TUT IS more famous for being dead than alive. He was a blip in Egyptian history until 1922, when some explorers hit pay dirt and found his three-thousand-year-old mummy nestled inside a giant sarcophagus. That sounds like a human body part, but it's just a fancy word meaning a stone box for a dead body. These grave-robbing explorers broke into Tut's tomb and took all his gold. And there was a lot of it because King Tut definitely planned on being king in the afterlife. What he didn't plan on was being probed, sliced, dismembered, X-rayed, scanned, and drilled for his DNA.

Pictures of a bird, two hooks, a comb, an arrow, a sandal strap, and a couple of speed bumps spell Tutankhamun in hieroglyphics. Today, we just call him King Tut. He is also called the Boy King. He got to be the king of Egypt when he was nine years old. He was only ten when he married Ankhsenamun, who unfortunately was his half sister, which was okay back then but would be really wrong now. Besides ruling Egypt, Tut did regular kid things like riding in chariots, throwing sticks, and firing his slingshot.

And then, *poof*, he died.

Even though Tut had died, he wasn't finished. Ancient Egyptians believed there is a life after this one, so after his death Tut's corpse was prepped for life number two. He was given the seventy-day royal mummy treatment.

So that Tut wouldn't rot on the trip to the next life, the embalmers scooped his insides out from top to bottom. To get his brains out, a long bronze needle with a hook on the end was shoved up his nose. His brain was broken up into teeny bits and pulled out one piece at a time. The Egyptians believed the brain's only job was to keep the ears apart, and that the heart did all the thinking.

They didn't take Tut's teeth, nails, and eyeballs. They left Tut's heart in his body because he was going to need that to think. And they left his genitals so no one would mistake him for Queen Tut.

Next, they cut open Tut's stomach and pulled out whatever they could get their hands on—like his liver, stomach, lungs, and twenty-two feet of intestines. Everything was washed, dried, put into four jars, and wrapped to go with him.

They covered Tut's altered corpse with natron (saltlike stuff) and put it on a slanted board with grooves in it so his bodily fluids flowed directly into a tub at the end. His gutted body was completely dried, which was especially difficult considering the human body is 75 percent water. They stuffed his chest with wads of cloth to soak up the inside juice. Every weensy drop of blood, rag, and leftover bit of Tut was saved and crammed into big jars for him to take along for his next excellent adventure.

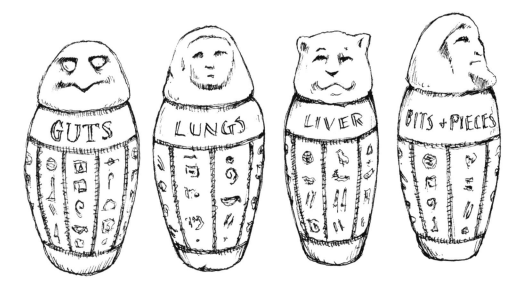

Tut's cadaver gave new meaning to the words "stiff" and "stinky," so it was smeared with scented goo to make it smell better and to make it feel less like Tut jerky.

Then, to make him look like a real mummy and to keep him from falling apart during a ceremony when a priest stood him up and offered him grapes, Tut's pruned corpse was encased by half a football field worth of fabric strips spun around his body like cotton candy, along with 143 charms woven in for good luck. To seal everything, they poured warmed plant resin (sap) all over Tut's wrapped body. Think superglue.

Meanwhile, servants picked up a few of his kingly things from the palace, including a couple of thrones, two slingshots, two jars of honey, six chariots, thirty golden statues, thirty-five model boats, 130 walking sticks, 427 arrows, and lots of sandals.

When Tut died, no one in Egypt had built a pyramid for a dead king for two hundred years because tomb raiders had trashed every single one of them, taking everything—including the mummies. Tomb raiders took off with the mother lode of ancient Egyptian history.

So they buried Tut in a tomb hidden under a sand dune in the middle of the desert known as the Valley of the Kings.

And there he rested undisturbed for three thousand years.

In 1922, Howard Carter—an English guy who had been digging around the Valley for twenty years—found Tut's intact tomb under a trillion grains of sand. Carter took ten years to pick through Tut's personal things and divvy them up to museums all over the world. The Egyptians told Carter, "Go home already."

But first Carter and his team did an "autopsy." It was hard to do

4

because Tut was superglued to the bottom of his coffin, and his famous gold mask was attached to his head. Carter managed to figure out Tut had been a teenager when he died because his teeth hadn't all come in yet and his leg bones weren't fully developed.

King Tut was returned to his sarcophagus and went nighty-night back in his tomb in the Valley of the Kings for about forty more years.

In 1968, experts X-rayed Tut's mummy to figure out how he had died. They noticed Tut's breastbone, genitals, one thumb, and a few ribs were missing. The X-rays also showed that his vertebrae were fused together and his skull was misshapen. They analyzed the facts and announced, "King Tut was murdered!"

Historians took the murder theory and fit the facts to the crime. Egyptologists had a new angle, history books were rewritten, and museum exhibits were revamped.

Tut stayed put for ten more years, until scientists removed him from his stone box again in 1978. He was still dead. They took more X-rays but never published their findings. And from a bone sample, they analyzed his blood. Tut's blood types were A2 and MN.

In 2005, there was new equipment to try out on Tut: a CT scan (way better than an X-ray). That was the first time anyone got a good look at what Carter forgot to mention after his so-called autopsy. He had broken off Tut's arms and legs and sliced Tut's chest down the middle. Carter also chiseled Tut's head off to get it free of the solid-gold mask. And to get Tut's 143 good-luck charms, Carter cut the body wrapping with an X-Acto blade. Afterward he glued Tut back together with wax and put the mangled mummy in a bed of sand. He didn't bother to reattach Tut's genitals, thumb,

5

and ribs; he just buried them in the sand. And then he put Tut back inside the coffin.

Carter was just another tomb raider after all.

The CT scan showed that Tut had an overbite, a small cleft palate, and a bend in his spine. But there was something else: Tut had a broken leg, and this one was not Carter's doing.

The Boy King got a new obit—"Tut died of a broken leg that got infected." He went back into his stone box—but not for long.

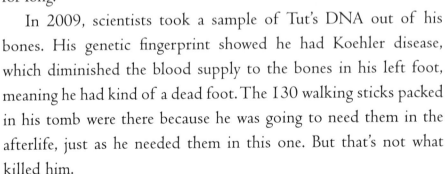

In 2009, scientists took a sample of Tut's DNA out of his bones. His genetic fingerprint showed he had Koehler disease, which diminished the blood supply to the bones in his left foot, meaning he had kind of a dead foot. The 130 walking sticks packed in his tomb were there because he was going to need them in the afterlife, just as he needed them in this one. But that's not what killed him.

Tut had malaria, a disease you get after being bitten by an infected mosquito. Malaria, along with his broken leg and dead foot, made for a dead king.

He died in 1323 BC. He was only nineteen years old. It didn't take a CT scan to see that Tut's leg was broken; it was visible to the naked eye and mentioned in Carter's original autopsy. It was also noted that Tut had a scabby, discolored indentation on the left side of his face. At the time, no one really knew what a three-thousand-year-old insect bite might look like, but now that we know Tut died of malaria, that scab on his face could be the mosquito bite that eventually killed him.

Tut's mummy is back in his tomb. Maybe now he can rest in peace. But for how long?

THINGS TO DO WITH OLD MUMMIES

PHARAOHS AND MILLIONS OF COMMON people were mummified in ancient times. Later, mummies were shipped by the ton all over the world for other uses, including:

1. MUMMY MEDICINE

For hundreds of years (1300–1800) doctors believed burned and pulverized mummies made into oils and powders could cure:

abscesses	paralysis
coughs	poisoning
epilepsy	rashes
fractures	ulcers
palpitations	

SIDE EFFECTS OF SWALLOWING MUMMY MEDICINE
- serious vomiting
- evil-smelling breath

2. MUMMY PAPER

Every mummy has at least thirty pounds of cloth around it. Used mummy cloth was made into brown butcher paper in the mid-1800s for packaging meat (unbeknownst to shoppers). But fairly soon, mummy paper was discontinued—after an outbreak of cholera among the workers at the paper mill.

3. MUMMY PAINT

Ground-up mummy produced a deep brown favored by Romantic painters (1790–1850). There were problems with this paint:

- It never dried.
- It dripped down the painting in hot weather.
- It contracted and cracked in cold weather.
- It ruined any color under, over, or near it.

MUMMY EYEBALLS

MUMMY EYE SOCKETS LOOK EMPTY, but they're not. Eyeballs shrink to almost nothing during the drying process. The empty-looking sockets were sometimes filled with cloth, onions, or stones and painted to look like eyeballs.

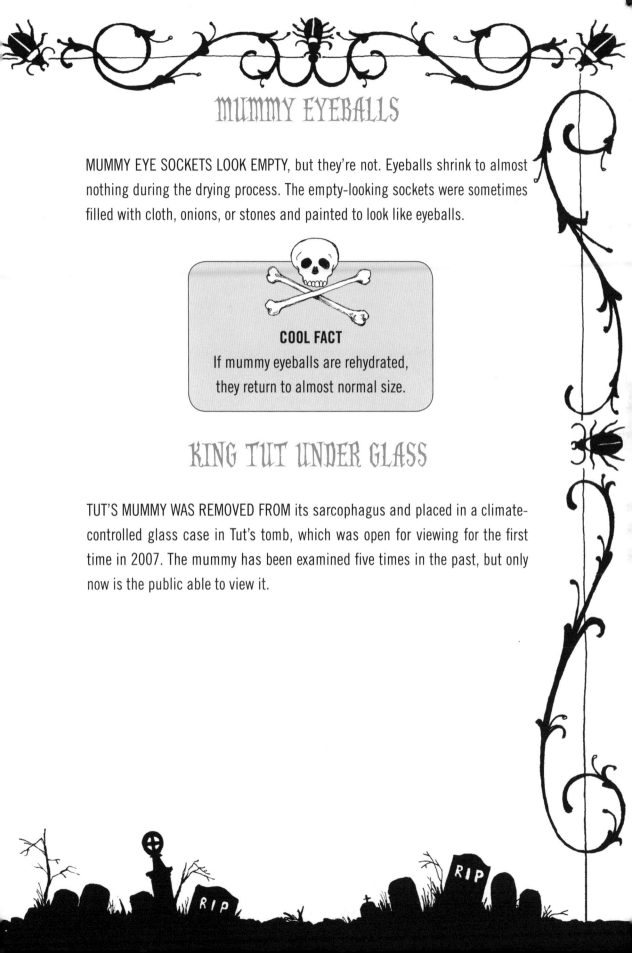

COOL FACT
If mummy eyeballs are rehydrated, they return to almost normal size.

KING TUT UNDER GLASS

TUT'S MUMMY WAS REMOVED FROM its sarcophagus and placed in a climate-controlled glass case in Tut's tomb, which was open for viewing for the first time in 2007. The mummy has been examined five times in the past, but only now is the public able to view it.

JULIUS CAESAR

PUTTING THE "I" IN "IDES"

Roman Statesman
Born: Rome, Italy,
July 13, 100 BC
Died: Rome, Italy,
March 15, 44 BC
56 years old

LIUS CAESAR WAS cut out of his mother, Aurelia Cotta, w
nife, during a medical birthing procedure that is known t
*caesar*ean section. It seems like it should have been cal
rean section (after his mom). But instead, Caesar got a
y. And that, in part, describes how Julius Caesar made hi
ugh life. Caesar was always saying I, I, I. "I came, I s
quered." And "I draw blood." Caesar survived fifty batt
off lands only to die in his hometown at the hands of po

riffraff in Rome. He left this world the same way he came into it—by the knife.

It was said, "He's tall for a Roman." That's code for not tall. Caesar was, however, intelligent, charismatic, and fast to action. He could rally crowds of men to grab their sandals and follow him off to sack yonder towns. His battle cry was "Happiness!" He loved everything military: the camping, the training, and the killing. Caesar paid his men well and made soldiering a real career.

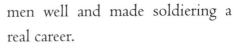

Caesar was into self-promotion before the concept was even invented. He wrote ten books about his fabulous life and called them history books. And he made his own birthday a holiday.

Caesar went to Egypt to take over the place, but he met Cleopatra and his plans changed. He kind of liked her, and he really liked all her gold. They had a son together. They called him Little Caesar, just like the pizza restaurant. Caesar had three wives, but none of them were Cleopatra.

The Roman Senate didn't want just one person to rule Rome, so Caesar was part of a three-man team called a triumvirate. That lasted a nanosecond because Caesar didn't like to share very much. After a civil war, Caesar said, "I am dictator for life," which was quite a horse pill for the senators to swallow, including Caesar's good friend Brutus.

Then Caesar said, "I'm Mr. Nice Dictator." He forgave his enemies, which was a big deal because normally it was so much easier to kill than to forgive. (Some people still feel that way.) Caesar lowered mortgage rates, gave away land, and built new settlements for veterans when they returned from war. The only thing was, he didn't pass these reforms by the Senate first.

The senators were just a bunch of rich guys and they wanted to keep everything for themselves. They decided that Caesar had to be stopped. He was getting too big for his toga and was a traitor to his class. Sixty senators, including his pal Brutus, hatched a plan. Caesar was scheduled to meet with the Senate on March 15, a date the Romans called the ides of March.

Legend has it Caesar decided to skip the Senate meeting because a fortune-teller had told him to "Beware the ides of March."

But then Brutus went to Caesar's house and acted all buddy-buddy to make sure Caesar would show up.

When Caesar entered the Senate hall, the conspirators moved in on him like hyenas circling a zebra they are about to eat for lunch.

One senator grabbed Caesar's robe and pulled it down off his shoulder, making Caesar's back an easy target for another senator to thrust his dagger into. Attacking Caesar from behind should have been a no-brainer, but the guy either was petrified or needed glasses because the knife barely grazed Caesar's shoulder. Within seconds, the wall of senators pulled hidden daggers from the pleats of their tunics. Caesar saw his friend Brutus and said, "You too, Brutus?"

Brutus started wildly swinging his dagger in Caesar's direction. All sixty senators were supposed to get a stab at Caesar so no one man could be blamed. Outnumbered sixty to one, even the great Caesar didn't stand a chance. He was stabbed in the legs, back, groin, face, and eyes. He pulled his toga up over his head and fell to the ground with twenty-three stab wounds. The remaining thirty-seven senators didn't need to bother.

The killers waited for Caesar to bleed to death on the floor. They didn't have a post-assassination strategy except to bolt out the door. Nobody wanted to be caught dead with a dead Caesar. The assassins thought they'd be heroes. Out in the streets, they proclaimed that Caesar was a tyrant and that Rome would be better off without him. But the citizens of Rome weren't buying it.

Caesar's body lay abandoned in a bloody heap for most of the day. Three servants eventually carried his remains to his house. Everybody came out to watch his bloody corpse go by.

Now an angry, seething crowd was forming. Military men who had served under Caesar were outside with their swords, ready to kill the assassins.

The murderous senators holed up together for the night and made a new plan while a riotous crowd took over Rome. The guilty and nervous senators decided to ratify all of Caesar's projects. They also decreed "Don't kill the assassins!" Nice decree.

A gilded shrine was constructed for Caesar's coffin in the center of town, and his murdered corpse was placed inside. The Romans went crazy.

Caesar's shrine was set on fire. Everything that wasn't nailed down was thrown in to stoke the fire. The gigantic funeral pyre burned for hours until only a mound of ashes was left.

Caesar had survived wars, battles, and treks to far-flung lands only to be killed in Rome, Italy, on March 15, 44 BC, by his peers. Beware the ides of March, indeed. He was fifty-six years old. In his will, Caesar gave his personal garden to the people of Rome, and he left money to every citizen.

The ides of March were bad luck for Caesar's assassins, too. Not one of them survived the next year; they were all hunted down and murdered.

AUTOPSY

THE FIRST RECORDED FORENSIC AUTOPSY—an examination of a dead body to find out the cause of death—was performed on Caesar.

Doctor Antistius determined that, of Caesar's twenty-three stab wounds, only the one in his chest was fatal. Caesar would have survived the other twenty-two.

Autopsies have been performed for thousands of years. Before the 1400s it was a crime to dissect a human body, but that didn't stop anatomy students, the so-called "body snatchers," from stealing corpses.

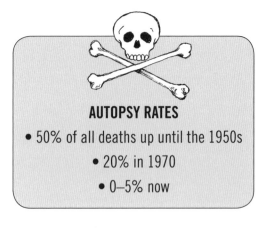

AUTOPSY RATES
- 50% of all deaths up until the 1950s
- 20% in 1970
- 0–5% now

In the 1500s, the Catholic Church accepted autopsies as a learning tool. Technological advancements like MRI (magnetic resonance imaging) and CT scans make most autopsies unnecessary today.

CALENDAR

THE ROMAN CALENDAR OF CAESAR'S time was only 355 days long. Ten days short per year quickly added up to snow in summer.

In 46 BC, Caesar made the year 365 days long—with an added day every fourth year, known as leap year. He named the new calendar after himself: the Julian calendar. But it was still eleven minutes off. In 1,600 years, those eleven minutes added up to snow in summer again.

In 1582, Pope Gregory XIII fixed the problem and put the snow back in winter once and for all with a new leap year rule. Years that are divisible by 4 *but not* by 100 are leap years. (It's a lot harder than it sounds.) He renamed it the Gregorian calendar, after himself. This is the calendar we use today.

THINGS NAMED AFTER CAESAR

July: Julius Caesar was born in the month of Quintilis; it was renamed July
Calendar: Julian calendar
Roman leaders: every Roman leader after him is named Caesar somebody or other
Czar: Russian leaders were named "Czar," which comes from "Caesar"
Kaiser: German leaders were named "Kaiser," which comes from "Caesar"
C-section: caesarean-section birth

THINGS NOT NAMED AFTER CAESAR

Caesar salad: originated in the 1920s by Caesar Cardini (of course, *he* was named after Julius Caesar)

CLEOPATRA

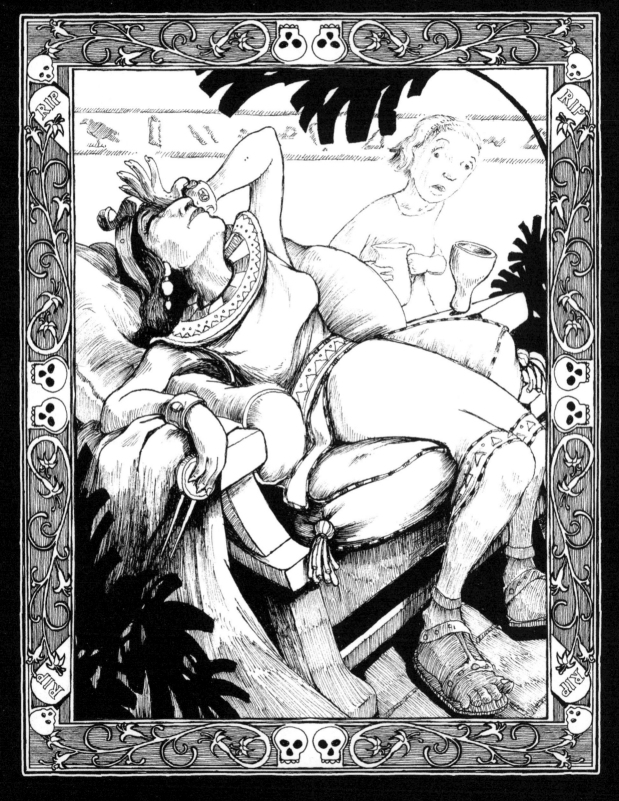

#1
ACROSS

Queen of Egypt
Born: Egypt,
69 BC
Died: Egypt,
August 12, 30 BC
39 years old

CLEOPATRA DIED OVER two thousand years ago, and still nobody can forget her. She was smart, ambitious, and glitzy. Her style was big, with a lot of bling. If you're a girl, it's fun to be her on Halloween, with her black eye makeup and distinctive hairdo.

Some people think they know how Cleopatra died because they do crossword puzzles. #1 Across: Cleopatra's killer, three letters. Answer: ASP. That rumor started because of the death scene in Shakespeare's play *Antony and Cleopatra*, which showed her aiming a

poisonous snake at her chest and arm. But the truth is, Cleopatra's death was more like the last scene in *Romeo and Juliet*.

Cleopatra's family had ruled Egypt for hundreds of years. Family members were known to marry, trick, and kill each other to get to the throne, and Cleopatra was no exception. She beat out five siblings for power and became queen at age eighteen.

Cleopatra knew everybody worth knowing in the first century BC. For a while she hung out with Julius Caesar—and even had a child with him—but that relationship was cut short when Caesar was assassinated.

Then she hung out with another Roman leader, Mark Antony. He turned out to be the love of her life. Like Romeo and Juliet, Antony and Cleopatra were secretly married—but their love affair lasted for years, until the day they died. She had three children with Mark Antony. Her love affairs with Caesar and Antony earned her the title the "Queen of Kings."

Besides being madly in love, Antony and Cleopatra had an insane desire to take over the world, including Rome. The Romans, led by Octavian, waged war against them. Antony and Cleopatra lost at the Battle of Actium, off the coast of Greece, but they survived. They split up to better their chances for survival.

Cleopatra ran for her life. It was only a matter of time before the Romans would catch her, kill her, and take over her beloved Egypt.

She hurried back home and started gathering every gold-headed figurine and gem-inlaid bowl she could get her hands on, not to mention all the royal jewelry, and stashed it in a mausoleum (tomb) she had built for herself in the royal cemetery.

When the Romans got to Egypt, she was ready. Cleopatra, her hairdresser, and her lady-in-waiting slipped inside the treasure-stuffed mausoleum and barricaded the doors. Every nook and cranny that wasn't full of gold was filled with firewood. Cleopatra had enough kindling to set the whole city on fire, starting with all the riches of Egypt sitting right there in the mausoleum. The Romans couldn't touch her.

Mark Antony, who was hiding someplace else, offered to kill himself to save Cleopatra from death. But nobody cared.

Then Antony received a message that Cleopatra was dead. Heartbroken, he stabbed himself in the stomach with his own sword. He was hanging on for dear life when another message arrived: *Please disregard the last message. Cleopatra is fine.* Antony was in no condition to travel, but he had a couple of men take him to the mausoleum so he could see for himself.

Before Antony got there, Cleopatra received a message that Antony was dead. So when Antony came banging on the mausoleum door, Cleopatra wouldn't let him in. She thought it was a trick. The women with Cleopatra saw Antony from an upper-story window, so they threw down ropes and hoisted Antony up and into the window.

Antony saw for himself that Cleopatra was alive. But then he died in her arms.

Clearly, there were major kinks in the way messages were sent back and forth, so Cleopatra didn't bother sending a message to the Romans that Antony was dead; she sent his bloody sword.

Turns out, Antony had given the Romans a good idea. They got themselves a ladder, climbed into the same mausoleum window that he had, and ambushed Cleopatra. She lunged for a dagger so she could stab someone—maybe herself—but more likely one of them. In any case, they wrested the knife out of her hands and she stabbed no one.

Because she was a woman, and also because it would be bad press for the new emperor, the Romans didn't kill Cleopatra. Their plan was to shackle her in chains and parade her in the streets of Rome. At best, she would spend the rest of her days as a sideshow attraction.

Cleopatra was placed under "palace arrest" while preparations were made for the trip to Rome. One night, Cleopatra, her hairdresser, and her lady-in-waiting were in the ex-queen's chambers having what must have looked like a slumber party. They dressed up and ordered a basket of fruit to be delivered to the room. Then Cleopatra sent the Romans a message asking to be buried next to Mark Antony when she died.

Gee, what did she mean by that?

The Romans charged into her room. Cleopatra was stretched out on a golden couch. There was no blood or sign of a struggle. She was dead. Expired at her feet was her lady-in-waiting. Her hairdresser was doing one last touch-up, placing a wreath of flowers on Cleopatra's head. Then she dropped dead, too.

The poison trade was big business in Egypt then, and toxic plants like aconite, henbane, and hemlock were easy to come by at your local pyramid. Cleopatra had two prick marks on her arm, not from the bite of a snake, but from a poisoned hairpin.

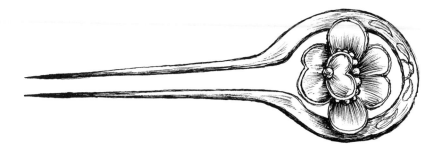

Cleopatra had been the queen of Egypt for twenty-one years. She was thirty-nine years old when she died on August 12, 30 BC. Egypt became part of the Roman Empire for the next four hundred years. Records say Cleopatra was buried with royal honors next to Mark Antony, but their tomb has never been found.

The message of how Cleopatra died got garbled over the past two thousand years. It should just be a matter of time before crossword puzzles are changed. #1 Across: Cleopatra's killer, six letters. Answer: POISON.

CROSSWORD-PUZZLE WORDS FOR "DEAD"

4 letters: cold, dull, gone
5 letters: inert, slain, quiet
6 letters: asleep, lapsed, *muerto*
7 letters: defunct, expired, extinct
8 letters: deceased, departed, lifeless, obsolete
9 letters: bloodless, inanimate, unfeeling
10 letters: breathless, lusterless, motionless, unexciting
11 letters: indifferent, ineffectual, inoperative
12 letters: extinguished, unproductive

CLEOPATRA'S KIDS

CAESAR AND CLEOPATRA'S SON
Caesarion: killed by Octavian, the man who defeated Cleopatra and Antony; Caesarion posed a threat because he could make a claim on the throne

ANTONY AND CLEOPATRA'S CHILDREN
Cleopatra Selene: married King Juba II of Numidia and Mauretania; had two children
Alexander Helios: disappeared
Ptolemy Philadelphus: disappeared

FAMOUS PEOPLE WHO WERE IMPRISONED OR CAPTURED

· CLEOPATRA ·
captured by Octavian after being defeated in the Battle of Actium

· RICHARD I (The Lionheart) ·
captured by King Leopold of Austria and held for two years,
until England raised the money for his ransom

· CHRISTOPHER COLUMBUS ·
arrested after third landing at Santo Domingo

· ELIZABETH I ·
arrested for plotting to overthrow her half sister, Bloody Mary

· POCAHONTAS ·
captured as leverage for the British settlers

· GALILEO GALILEI ·
arrested for writing a book about a sun-centered universe

· MARIE ANTOINETTE ·
arrested for being the queen of France during the French Revolution

· DANIEL BOONE ·
captured by the Shawnee, adopted by the tribe, and named Big Turtle until he
escaped four months later and warned settlers of an impending attack

· NAPOLEON BONAPARTE ·
arrested after losing a battle with the British

· NELSON MANDELA ·
imprisoned for twenty-seven years for trying to overthrow South Africa's
racist government; elected the first black president of
South Africa within a year of his release

CHRISTOPHER COLUMBUS

DEATH
BY DIRT

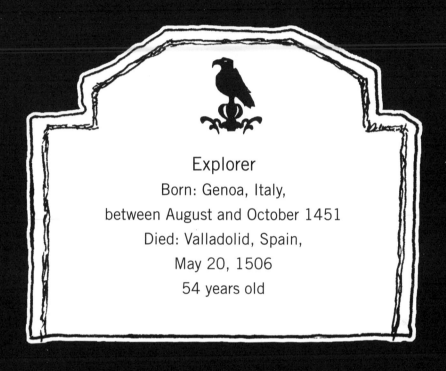

Explorer

Born: Genoa, Italy,
between August and October 1451
Died: Valladolid, Spain,
May 20, 1506
54 years old

AT SEA, CHRISTOPHER COLUMBUS had the magic touch. But on land, not so much. All he talked about was his dream to head east to the Orient, but he wanted to sail west to get there. Not a smart idea. Most people already thought the world was roundish, but what about all that upside-down water on the other side? Why on earth would he want to search for land by sailing in the wrong direction, eating bad food, and sleeping all squished in a tiny cabin? Everybody thought Columbus had sprung a leak. But Columbus had determination, and he was just nutty enough to attempt the stupidest idea anyone had ever heard. People with big dreams don't care where they sleep.

Columbus was born in Italy. He moved to Portugal, got married, had two sons, and tried to get the Portuguese royals there to bankroll his dream—but they said no. Columbus was so annoyed, he moved to Spain. For eight years, he pestered King Ferdinand and Queen Isabella of Spain to give him money to go exploring. Columbus had a plan: everything he discovered would belong to Spain, but he would get 10 percent of all the gold and spices.

The king and queen finally told Columbus to get off his knees and go find gold.

In 1492, one hundred men jammed into three ships: the *Niña*, the *Pinta*, and the *Santa María*. Columbus was forty-one years old. Things like a telescope, sunglasses, brimmed hats, and potties aboard ship hadn't been invented yet, so they headed west into unmapped waters short a bunch of basic stuff.

Some thought the trip would take three years, but Columbus was better than anyone at the helm of a ship. He read the wind, stared at the sun, and squinted at the horizon for only thirty-three days before he spotted land. It wasn't the Orient but it was land, and Columbus claimed it for Spain. He called it Hispaniola. The clothing-optional natives he encountered had gold rings in their noses—a very good sign. Columbus sailed home.

In Spain, that crazy Columbus was now a hero. Ferdinand and Isabella let him lead a second voyage, with seventeen ships, back to Hispaniola to drop off fifteen hundred men to start digging for gold.

But Columbus felt lousy en route. He had diarrhea, which wasn't exactly a picnic at sea. Going to the bathroom aboard ship meant hanging your butt off a plank out over the water, then wiping with a piece of rope dangling nearby. Poop germs got on everybody's hands, and since they used their hands to eat, it created a perfect storm of infections. Exposure to damp, chilly air for months on end made Columbus's joints stiff, swollen, and so painful he couldn't walk. He kept sailing around as best he could, but he couldn't find the Orient, and no one found any gold, either.

When Columbus sailed back to Spain, Ferdinand and Isabella were not happy with the news.

Columbus got out his knee pads again and begged for more time to find the Orient. But by now it seemed like Columbus couldn't find anything. His eyes were bloody from strain and sun exposure. His sea legs were gone because the shipboard diet of salted beef, pickled sardines, and wine had given him gout, which made his feet swell. He was a shipwreck himself.

In spite of this, Columbus got funding to go on more voyages. He found the New World by landing in Venezuela. But he couldn't see it or step foot on it himself because his vision was blurry and spotted with dark blobs, and he

29

was hunched over with arthritis. His hands looked like claws, and the sunlight aggravated his swollen, bleeding eyes. A cabin was built specially for him on the main deck because he could barely navigate his own body. The ship was a floating bed for Columbus.

Even though Columbus was crippled and sailing blind, he and his crew found land at the site where the Panama Canal would be built centuries later. The Pacific Ocean was only thirty-two miles away on the other side of the land. Columbus would have liked that; the Pacific Ocean could take him to the Orient. But it was too late. As if things weren't bad enough, Columbus caught malaria, a disease spread by mosquitoes. He had chills, a fever, and difficulty breathing. His navigational antennae were all but broken, causing him and his crew to get shipwrecked in Jamaica. It took a year before one of his men safely canoed to Hispaniola and arranged a rescue.

Almost dead, Columbus barely made it back to Spain. He moved into a monastery where he was taken care of by friars, who couldn't refuse anyone, even crazy sailors. Columbus worked on the plans for his next voyage. But that would be just a dream.

Columbus died on May 20, 1506; he was fifty-four years old. No one came to his funeral. It didn't get mentioned in the newspaper. Isabella was dead, and Ferdinand had no intention of paying Columbus's 10 percent to his family, so no one was allowed even to say Columbus's name. His family eventually sold off all his maps and letters.

Columbus wasn't given credit for finding the New World. Amerigo

Vespucci was a passenger on a trip to the New World in 1499. He wrote a book claiming he had discovered it, which was a big fat lie. A mapmaker read his book, and he named the New World "America" after Amerigo. That name stuck like glue. At least the mapmaker didn't name it "Vespucca."

History forgot about Columbus for three hundred years. In the 1800s, the king of Spain took Columbus's logbooks out of the royal archives, and Columbus finally got credit for finding the New World.

Over the years, Columbus's remains took a few voyages, too. First he was buried in Spain. Then records show that his family took his remains to Hispaniola, the island that today holds the countries of Haiti and the Dominican Republic. Years later, his body was taken to Cuba. These countries all still claim to have Columbus's bones.

By doing DNA tests on his bones, scientists confirmed that at least some of Columbus's remains are in Spain. Cuba, Haiti, and the Dominican Republic declined to have their Columbus caches tested.

Recently, doctors have concluded from Columbus's symptoms that he died of Reiter's syndrome. It's a rare disease people get from living in tight quarters where there is bad hygiene—a disease that some soldiers, sailors, and marines still get today. It starts with dysentery and then attacks the eyes, joints, and urinary tract.

If you have a dream, and it's in your guts to do it, don't worry if there might be tight quarters, and don't take no for an answer. But don't forget the soap.

31

SCURVY: THE SAILOR KILLER

IN 1564, THE DUTCH NOTICED that eating oranges made symptoms disappear. Two hundred years later a Scottish surgeon noticed that all citrus fruits did the same.

In 1795, the British Royal Navy added lime juice to daily rations, which is why British sailors are nicknamed "limeys."

SCURVY
is a disease that killed more than 100,000 sailors at sea. The symptoms are extreme exhaustion, bleeding gums, and death.

A healthy British navy was a contributing factor in the victory over Napoleon.

In 1928, vitamin C was identified in all citrus fruits. Sailors with scurvy lacked vitamin C.

MAPPING MAPS

150 AD

Ptolemy drew twenty-six maps with India where America is. That's why Columbus thought he had reached India (when he had actually discovered a new place not on any map) and why Native Americans were called Indians.

1492

First globe of earth, missing the soon-to-be-discovered Americas and the Pacific Ocean

GOUT

GOUT IS CAUSED BY A deposit of sharp crystals in the joints. The crystals form when there's an abnormally high concentration of uric acid in the blood.

Crystals are minute, splinter-sharp fragments that can form overnight, followed by shivering and fever. They most often attack the big toe, but the heel, the calf, and the ankle are also targets. Half of gout sufferers have kidney stones, too.

Gout causes severe agony. It even hurts to wear shoes or clothes.

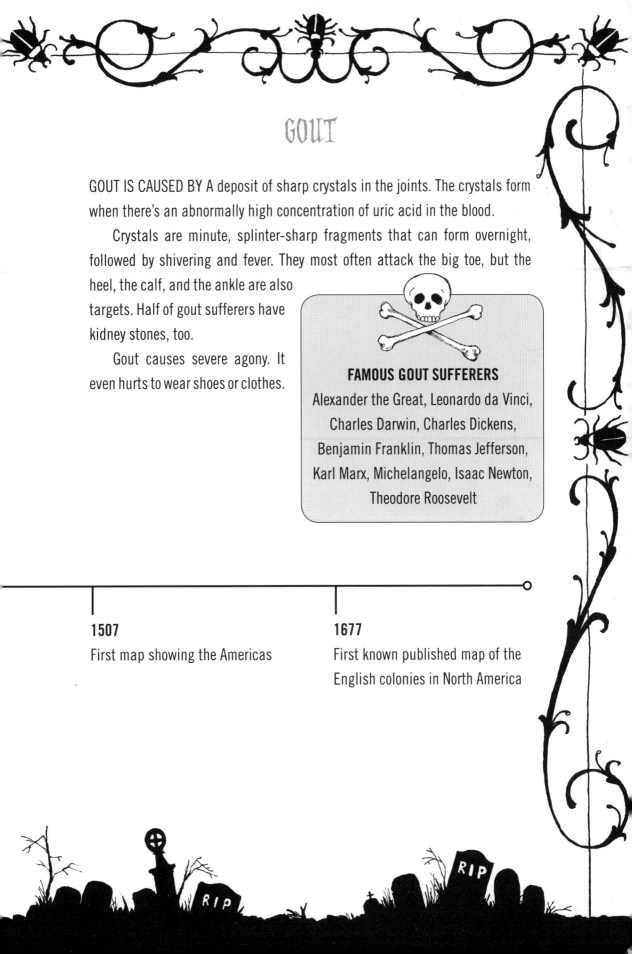

FAMOUS GOUT SUFFERERS

Alexander the Great, Leonardo da Vinci, Charles Darwin, Charles Dickens, Benjamin Franklin, Thomas Jefferson, Karl Marx, Michelangelo, Isaac Newton, Theodore Roosevelt

1507
First map showing the Americas

1677
First known published map of the English colonies in North America

HENRY VIII

WHO NOT TO MARRY

King of England
Born: London, England,
June 28, 1491
Died: London, England,
January 28, 1547
55 years old

HENRY VIII BECAME the king of England when he was a hormonally charged seventeen-year-old. Gifted in jousting and wrestling, Henry was loved for his youthful prowess. His subjects adored him until his murdering ways changed their minds. Henry turned out to be an evil thinker. He wasn't nice to anyone, not even himself. One gobblefest after another of supersized feasts and troughs of wine, and Henry VIII transformed himself from a beautiful young king into Humpty Dumpty. And he had a great fall.

Writing music and collecting bejeweled doublets were jolly pastimes for the king, along with festooning London Bridge with the skulls of his beheaded victims.

Six lucky ladies got to be his queen at different times, but not one kept the tiara for long. In an era when name originality was low, he married three Katherines, two Annes, and a Jane. The first Anne and the second Katherine got their heads on the bridge. He divorced the first Katherine and the second Anne. Jane died in childbirth, and the third Katherine outlived him. With the various queens, he had two daughters and a son.

Killing seventy thousand of his countrymen just because they didn't agree with him, bankrupting the Treasury, and burying all those wives made Henry want to overeat until his outsides matched who he was on the inside—a hateful, 320-pound ogre.

The blood in His Largeness's legs had trouble circulating back to his heart past all that fat, and a throbbing, purplish, stinky open wound of rotting flesh, pus, plugged veins, and exposed nerve endings developed on his thigh. It caused him excruciating pain and high fevers. All the king's horses and all the king's men put together mixtures of lead, silver, pulverized coral, and "dragon's blood" (whatever that was), cooked it into a paste, and smeared it on his leg. They made the king drink ground pearls and sawdust mixed with water. Whenever the skin healed over the infection, it hurt Henry even more and his doctors would start over again.

"The king's sore leg" was not open for discussion. His spies were ordered to report people chitchatting about the king's health. The punishment was to have their ears cut off or to be burned at the stake—king's choice. So everywhere the king went, mum was the word. There was an elephant in the room, and it was Henry.

At forty-four, he jousted for the last time. Dressed in full-body armor, limping and clanking, he climbed the specially made platform to mount his horse, which was also clad in full regalia. The king and his ride were a humongous and easy target. It was always best to let the king win, but this time, with only 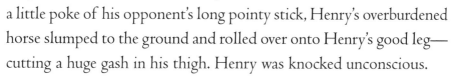 a little poke of his opponent's long pointy stick, Henry's overburdened horse slumped to the ground and rolled over onto Henry's good leg—cutting a huge gash in his thigh. Henry was knocked unconscious.

Henry's horse was the only living thing brave enough to let the king know the truth about his bulk.

Everybody thought it might be the end of King Henry, but no one was talking, which was good thinking because two hours later he woke up.

Things were normal for a while, until Henry went on a trip to shoot spears and darts at stags. He returned bloated and feverish, with both legs inflamed. He could barely walk. All the king's horses and all the king's men didn't dare say the king was on the brink of death. Instead, they collected his urine in flasks so they could compare it to the amount of liquid he drank. The doctors examined his stools and gave him enemas to lower his fever. Whatever they were being paid, it wasn't enough.

Barber-surgeons, who were trained to cut hair, lance boils, pull teeth, and perform other minor yet painful procedures, cauterized Henry's legs. Burning hot irons were applied to his leg wounds. The treatment melted away the flesh to stop the bleeding and halt the spread of infection. Except it didn't work. Henry VIII died on January 28, 1547, from infected legs and not enough blood getting to his lungs (called a pulmonary embolism). He was fifty-five years old.

For two days, still afraid to talk, no one spilled the beans that the king was dead. His meals were delivered with the trumpets blaring and the usual whoop-de-do while Henry was dead in his bed, smelling like a giant rotting egg.

Eventually he was placed in a not-so-completely-sealed lead coffin. While lying in state, it is believed that his toxic remains exploded, and some of his royal splendidness dripped out the sides of the coffin overnight.

The body of Henry VIII was buried in a vault in St. George's Chapel, next to the body of his third wife, Queen Jane, the mother of his only son. (She probably wasn't that glad for

38

the company.) After Henry was put to rest, no one bothered to finish the vault or even put his name on it.

In 1649, the chapel was partially dismantled during the Great Rebellion. And in 1805, the stone sarcophagus was taken away and used by someone else. In 1813, Henry VIII's unmarked vault was found completely by accident. His coffin, which was never sealed properly, was partially open. Maybe it had finally aired out some. Later, Queen Victoria refurbished the chapel in memory of Prince Albert. It was renamed the Albert Memorial Chapel. Henry VIII's tomb is there.

FEASTING AT THE PALACE

EATEN IN ONE DAY BY HENRY VIII AND HIS COURT (ABOUT 1,200 PEOPLE):

11 cows

17 hogs

6 sheep

450 chickens

6 cranes

72 geese

648 larks

4 peacocks

384 pigeons

15 swans

1,300 apples

3,000 pears

3,000 loaves of bread

THINGS THAT WEIGH AS MUCH AS HENRY VIII

- 58,060 U.S. pennies
- 244 regulation basketballs
- Jabba the Hutt

QUEEN FOR A DAY

HENRY'S WIVES	TIME WEARING TIARA	REASON ENDED
Katherine of Aragon	23 years 11 months	Divorced
Anne Boleyn	3 years 4 months	Beheaded
Jane Seymour	1 year 10 months	Died in childbirth
Anne of Cleves	6 months	Divorced
Katherine Howard	1 year 7 months	Beheaded
Katherine Parr	3 years 6 months	Widowed

ELIZABETH I

SHE KEPT HER HEAD ABOUT HER

Queen of England
Born: London, England,
September 7, 1533
Died: London, England
March 24, 1603
69 years old

ELIZABETH WAS A princess. Her father, Henry VIII, was enraged she wasn't a prince. Elizabeth knew this because he beheaded her mother, Anne Boleyn, in part because she gave birth to a girl. That kind of thing makes an impression. Several years later, he beheaded her stepmother, too. So being a princess was scary. Elizabeth liked her head and she wanted to keep it. At eight she said, "I will never marry." Elizabeth orchestrated her life so that no man could ever take her head in a violent, bloody death.

Elizabeth's older stepsister, Mary, was queen before her. Her nickname was "Bloody Mary." They didn't have family barbecues, but Mary did enjoy burning Protestants at the stake. Luckily for everybody, Mary died and Elizabeth became the queen of England.

The red-haired Elizabeth was twenty-five years old when the coronation ring was placed on her long, narrow finger. Now that she was queen, her advisers set her up on dates and told her to get a husband, have an heir, and then she'd be safe. She liked men and they liked her—but she liked her head more.

"I am already bound unto an husband, which is the kingdom of England," she announced. The bachelorette queen became known as Elizabeth the Great. She was also known as the Virgin Queen, although the truth of that title cannot be confirmed.

Beside being witty, smart, and charismatic, Elizabeth had simple strategies for success: save the country from bankruptcy; own three thousand dresses; use the chopping block sparingly; wear miles of pearls; dance, dance, dance; avoid war like the plague; and use skin-whitening lotion made of egg whites, powdered eggshell, alum, borax, and poppy seeds.

Like father, like daughter. Elizabeth did a few un-great things: beheading the Duke of Norfolk, Mary Queen of Scots, and the Earl of

Essex, even though she had her reasons. On the other hand, she stopped the Spanish Armada from invading England. That was truly great!

Except for the occasional rotten tooth, and a pesky open sore on her shin that didn't heal for nine years, Elizabeth enjoyed an uncommonly long and healthy life with her head still attached. But at sixty-nine, Elizabeth's body was starting to show signs of wear and tear. Whose wouldn't? She was forgetful, and her joints were swollen and painful. The coronation ring that had been placed on her thin finger forty-four years earlier when she became queen was getting hard to see on her swollen finger. It was hurting her, and the ring had to be sawed off—an event disturbing to Elizabeth as a symbol that her reign was almost over and that her fingers weren't pretty anymore. She never went out in public again.

Elizabeth's doctor read the horoscope for her birth sign, Virgo. In 1603, a "medico-astrological chart" was one of the few items in a doctor's kit, along with a knife, a flint, and a cup. Elizabeth's horoscope said the stars were in her favor.

But the horoscope stars were wrong. Her throat was closing up with an infection and sores, and she had a high fever. She had trouble moving around, but the queen refused to get into bed. The bed symbolized the end to her—

45

and she was not ready for that—so cushions were spread on the floor, and there she sat. Elizabeth stared off into space for hours at a time with a finger stuck in her mouth. Maybe it was the finger they sawed the ring off, or maybe it was the finger with the sapphire ring she knew they'd remove when she was dead—the ring they'd give to the next king.

Elizabeth stayed on the floor and refused to be treated by her doctors. No one was going to interfere with the kind of death she had in mind for herself. She wasn't going to lose her head.

Her chief minister advised her, "Your Worship must returneth to bed."

"Little man, the word 'must' is not to be used to princes," Elizabeth said.

The queen's cousin Robert Carey came from out of town, and tried to cheer her up by telling her she looked better.

That made Elizabeth mad, and she squeezed his hand hard. "No, I'm not well." She knew it was Carey's job to wiggle the sapphire ring off her finger as soon as she stopped breathing and deliver it to the next king. She was not losing her marbles.

The pus-filled sores in her throat made it impossible to eat, and now her stomach hurt, too. Finally, she asked to be helped off the floor so she could stand up. All told, she had been resting on the floor cushions for three weeks. Everybody was thrilled she was up. But then Elizabeth stood in exactly the same position for fifteen hours straight.

A big sore in her throat popped and she felt better, but not for long. The infection moved into her chest. The failing queen *finally* got into bed. She summoned her musicians to play music softly around her while she lay there, not eating or talking.

46

Archbishop Whitgift came and knelt next to the bed, taking hold of her hand. The archbishop was old like Elizabeth, and he is famous for his dedication at her bedside. The pain in his legs became so prickly and sharp from kneeling that he tried to leave several times. But Elizabeth made it clear he needed to stay put and pray for her soul. As a result, his prayers took on new, fiery zeal. "God have mercy!" While his enthusiasm rose, Elizabeth closed her eyes and fell asleep.

At three o'clock in the morning of March 24, 1603, Queen Elizabeth died the death of her dreams—in her sleep. She was sixty-nine years old. She most likely died of pneumonia.

A lady-in-waiting removed the sapphire ring from Elizabeth's finger and dropped it out the window to Carey, who was below, already saddled up on a horse. He rode like the wind for three days to get to Scotland and gave the ring to Elizabeth's first cousin once removed, who then became the new king of England, James I.

The queen's body was embalmed and placed in a lead coffin. One month later, she was buried in the vault of her grandfather King Henry VII, in Westminster Abbey. In 1606, her body was moved to a tomb under a large white marble monument in the north aisle. To this day, she is still considered the most popular and effective monarch England has ever had.

Elizabeth I was a model for women of power in the future. She took the reign, wore the ring, and kept her head.

47

SHAKESPEARE PLAYS WRITTEN DURING THE REIGN OF ELIZABETH I

As You Like It • *The Comedy of Errors*

Hamlet • *Julius Caesar*

A Midsummer Night's Dream • *Much Ado About Nothing*

Richard III • *Romeo and Juliet*

Twelfth Night

BONEYARD WORDS

Coffin: box for a dead body

Crypt: chamber underneath a church used as a burial place

Sarcophagus: stone coffin

Shrine: cabinet or chest enclosing an honored dead person

Tomb: enclosure dug into the earth or rock for a corpse

Vault: burial chamber that is usually partially or entirely underground

A FEW OF THE PEOPLE BURIED OR COMMEMORATED IN WESTMINSTER ABBEY

William Blake	Robert Browning
Lewis Carroll	Geoffrey Chaucer
Sir Winston Churchill	Charles Darwin
Charles Dickens	George Handel
Samuel Johnson	Martin Luther King Jr.
Sir Isaac Newton	William Shakespeare

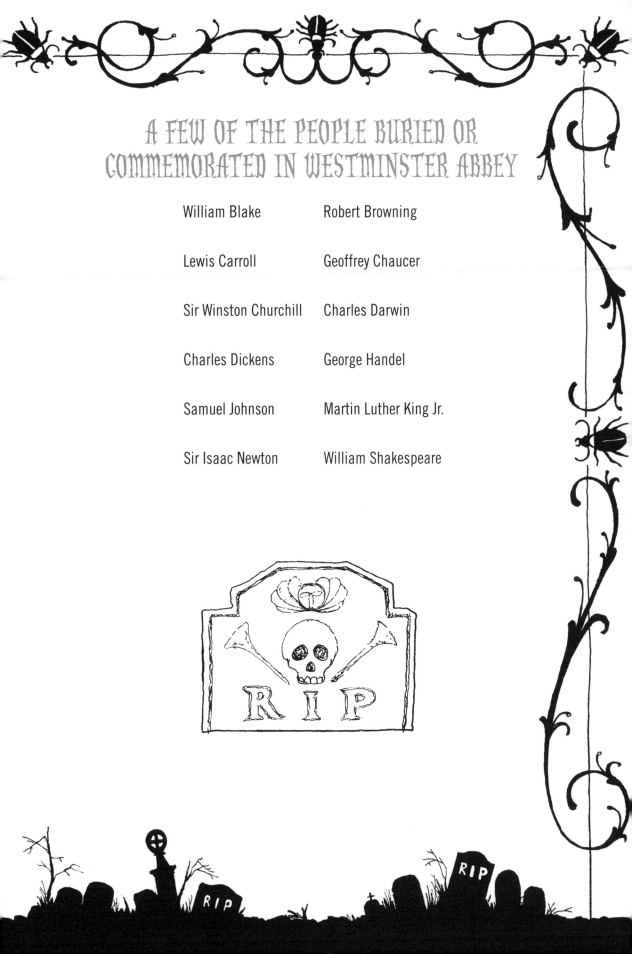

POCAHONTAS

ROYAL HOSTAGE

Native American Princess
Born: Virginia,
circa 1596
Died: Gravesend, England,
March 21, 1617
21 years old

POCAHONTAS WAS A Native American princess. She was the daughter of Chief Powhatan. Today, "princess" can mean "spoiled brat," and even though she was the real deal, the name "Pocahontas" actually means "spoiled child" in her language—so maybe things haven't changed all that much. But for sure, her life wasn't anything like what we've seen in the movies showing Pocahontas and John Smith, the English settler, as being practically engaged.

Pocahontas was only eleven years old when she met Smith, and he left the New World two years later. No one likes mentioning what really happened to Pocahontas. It went like this: she was used, duped, captured, taken to England, and exhibited as living, breathing proof that "savages" could be civilized—except Pocahontas wasn't living and breathing for long.

Her early life was idyllic. She skipped here and there around her lush digs with their ponds, woods, and maize-on-the-cob, in what was eventually known as the state of Virginia. Things were perfect until a bunch of Englishmen, including Smith, came ashore in 1607 with plans to "civilize" the natives and seize everything in sight.

Chief Powhatan fought the settlers and took their guns. He was on the brink of beating John Smith's brains out when, according to Smith, Pocahontas threw herself over Smith and saved his life. The chief allowed Smith to live after he promised the chief that no more settlers would be coming—which we know was a lie because John Smith turned out to be the first of a gazillion John Smiths eventually to live in Virginia.

Pocahontas was delighted the killing had stopped. The young peacemaker made sure the Englishmen ate and smiled. But then more settlers arrived, and Smith left the colony without even a thank you. So she stopped helping the settlers. And without Pocahontas, there was no peace. You guessed it: fighting ensued.

Naturally, the settlers wanted their guns back. So they kidnapped Pocahontas and held her for ransom. She was seventeen years old. But Chief Powhatan didn't trade arms for hostages. So instead, the settlers took her to another colony fifty miles away to be "civilized." They taught her English and told her about important things like Christmas and guilt. She was trapped. You can bet they never taught her how to say "I want to go home now." They baptized her, renamed her Lady Rebecca, and married her off to John Rolfe, the luckiest guy in Virginia. Rolfe got Pocahontas's land (land came with the package when an Indian princess got married, even a kidnapped one) and he planted tobacco all over it. They had a son named Thomas.

Pocahontas couldn't escape. She was scared to death, completely made over from a deerskin-clad outdoorsy girl into a corset-and-bonnet-wearing indoor lady. Rolfe liked what he saw and decided to take Pocahontas and son to England on a promo tour, so he could get more money for the colony and for his tobacco farm.

One look at London, and Pocahontas knew why the English were moving to Virginia. London was a crowded, filthy, stinky eyesore. Human and animal waste were everywhere. The river Thames was full of garbage. The English bathed only once a year at that time, unlike the Indians who got wet every day. Sooty smoke from coal fires hovered in a yellow murky cloud above the city. The cloud blocked the sunlight. It was so . . . well . . . uncivilized.

Pocahontas was paraded around London and became a celebrity. She met King James I and raised funds for the Virginia colony that had kidnapped her. Everybody was happy except Pocahontas. She began to cough from the filthy air. At the time, London was a giant petri dish of germs. Without immunities to these foreign germs, she was like a sheep to the slaughter.

Pocahontas left London for a cleaner location in the English countryside. But she was still having trouble breathing. No one knew exactly what she was suffering from, but she was "in decline."

After waiting months for good sailing weather, Rolfe couldn't wait to get back to his tobacco farm. It didn't matter that Pocahontas was barely breathing. She was loaded aboard his ship, along with their two-year-old son, who was also ill.

But they didn't get far. The cold sea air turned the tide for Pocahontas; she probably turned blue. The ship docked at the town of Gravesend, and Pocahontas went ashore to get medical attention. However, there is no record that a doctor ever helped her—no surprise, given that the doctor–patient ratio at the time was one doc to every eight thousand people.

The next thing everybody knew, Pocahontas was dead. She died on March 21, 1617, in Gravesend. She died of either tuberculosis or pneumonia. She was only twenty-one years old.

54

So much for being a celebrity. News of her death wasn't even printed in the newspaper. Pocahontas's corpse was loaded into a coffin that day and taken down the block to St. George's Church. She was buried in a vault without any markings or headstone. Many years later, the church burned down. The only thing that survived the fire was the church's register of burials, with Pocahontas's name in it.

Instead of taking two-year-old Thomas back to Virginia with him, Rolfe left him to be nursed back to health and raised by his brother, Henry. Rolfe had what he wanted: land and the money to keep farming tobacco. Father and son never saw each other again.

Pocahontas believed in diplomacy; she did everything possible to foster peace between her people and the settlers. But her life was cut short by the manipulation of others. The deception and the filth did her in—so much for "civilization."

Pocahontas's son, Thomas, recovered, grew up, moved to Virginia, got married, and had a daughter. By the time Thomas got to Virginia, his dad was dead. Today, there are three million descendants of Pocahontas in England, the United States, and all over the world.

THE MANY NAMES OF POCAHONTAS

Pocahontas: childhood nickname meaning "spoiled child"

Matoaka: adult Indian name meaning "white bird"

Amonute: sacred priestess name used in ceremonies

Lady Rebecca: Christian name from an Old Testament story about a beautiful and wholesome foreign girl; given to her by English settlers

POCAHONTAS'S KIDNAPPING

POCAHONTAS WAS KIDNAPPED AND TAKEN fifty-five miles upriver to the fenced-in town of Henrico. Religion was the main focus there. Twice-daily church attendance was mandatory, and punishment for noncompliance was severe.

Missed once: no food for a week

Missed twice: flogged

Missed often: shot, hanged, or burned at the stake

CAPTAIN SAMUEL ARGALL

CAPTAIN SAMUEL ARGALL WAS THE English ship captain who kidnapped Pocahontas by tricking her into boarding his ship.

Argall was captain of the ship on which Pocahontas was taken to London, where colonists hoped to use her to raise more money for the colony.

Argall was also captain of the ship the sick and dying Pocahontas boarded for the return trip to Virginia. Pocahontas died before they got out to sea.

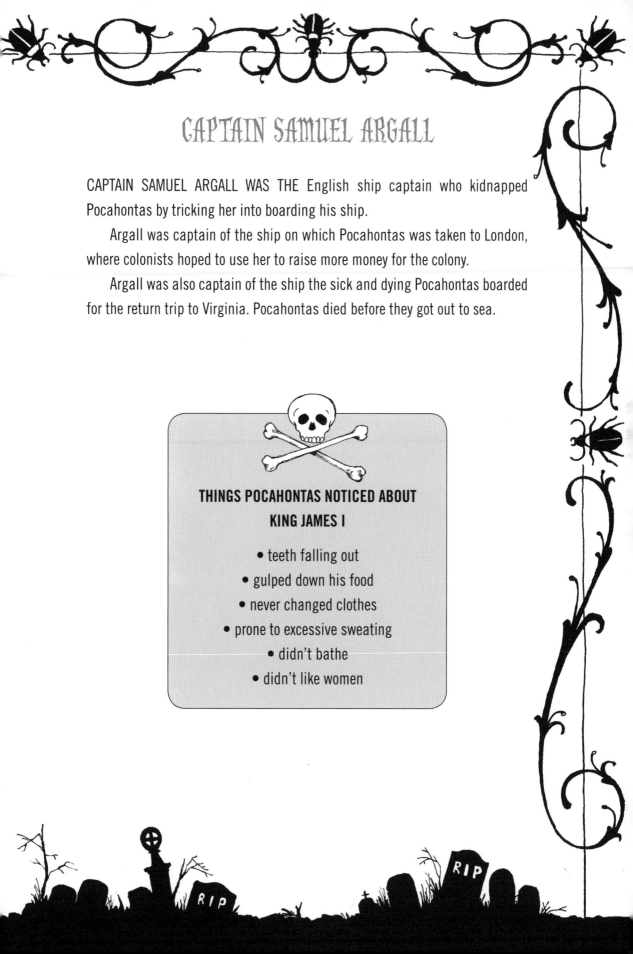

THINGS POCAHONTAS NOTICED ABOUT KING JAMES I

- teeth falling out
- gulped down his food
- never changed clothes
- prone to excessive sweating
- didn't bathe
- didn't like women

STAYING ALIVE

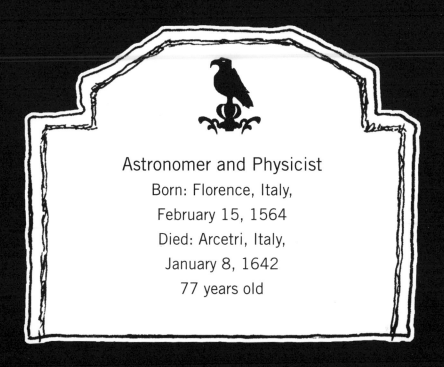

Astronomer and Physicist
Born: Florence, Italy,
February 15, 1564
Died: Arcetri, Italy,
January 8, 1642
77 years old

GALILEO WAS THE smartest guy in the room. He knew this, and so did everybody else. Most people couldn't even read and were just trying to get food on the table while Galileo was walking around asking himself questions like "What is the speed of falling things?" and "How can I calculate longitude at sea?" Then he'd figure out the answers himself.

Galileo thought the earth spun around the sun. The teachings of the Catholic Church were against the idea of the earth moving, and thinking something like what Galileo thought could get a person killed back then. But it took a lot to kill Galileo.

He was a mathematics professor for twenty years. In his day, professors lived with their students. Galileo gave out entertaining assignments like "Why does ice float in wine?" And then he drank the experiment. He figured out how to make a military compass that ensured cannonballs hit their targets. Galileo, the big man on campus, eventually became known the world over as "the father of modern science."

Galileo was also the biological father of three illegitimate children. He never married, and the mother of his children died young. He sent his two daughters to a nunnery, and his son went to law school.

In the 1500s, nobody lived long. If you made it to thirty-five years of age you were lucky. Because of plagues, poxes, and every other unimaginable nightmare that doctors didn't know how to cure, people dropped like flies.

At forty-five, when Galileo had outlived most of his peers, he got his hands on the first telescope, which didn't work much better than squinting through a paper-towel roll. He improved it to the magnification of thirty, about as powerful as one you can find today in any toy store. Then he pointed the thing at the sky—and actually discovered something.

It was common knowledge that Jupiter existed, but Galileo was the first to see Jupiter's four moons, and he also saw dark spots on the sun. Watching all these heavenly bodies, Galileo realized something was moving: us! The earth was moving around the sun.

In his own body, something else was moving—his kidney stones. Crystallized uric acid slowly came out through his urine and it felt like there were burning asteroids in his groin. The problem was, Galileo drank wine and never water. At the time, wine was considered safer to drink than water. More burning meteorites developed in his feet and knees, which was a disease called gout. It deformed his hands into claws with lumpy knuckles, twisted fingers, and raw skin. It didn't matter how smart he was; he didn't know that the lead added to his wine as flavoring was poisonous, as was the lead that leached from the metal casks the wine was cured in. He drank a lot of lead-laced wine. It gave him headaches, anemia, and rotten teeth.

Galileo was barely getting around when he sat down to write his book about the sun-centered universe, called *Dialogue Concerning the Two Chief World Systems.* He had a hole in his stomach muscle where his intestine bulged out, called a hernia. A heavy iron contraption called a truss was strapped on him every day to plug the hole. He saw a large halo around any light he looked at, and within the halo he saw nothing because of eye infections and what we now know as glaucoma.

None of this stopped him from writing. But what was he thinking? The last guy who mentioned a sun-centered universe was burned at the stake by the church police, the Holy Office of the Inquisition. The Inquisition had the power to hunt down people who believed something different from the teachings of the Catholic Church. These people were called heretics, and sometimes they were tortured and put to death.

61

Still, Galileo published his book. He believed it would be his ticket to immortality.

The leaders of the Inquisition called Galileo in for a trial. Who did he think he was?

When Galileo got to the trial, he was definitely the smartest guy in the room. But that wouldn't impress the inquisitors, so he played dumb. That didn't stop them from finding him guilty of heresy (rejecting the beliefs of those in power). He was sentenced to death, as a lesson to others. But Galileo was smart enough to know he didn't need to die to make the truth *more true*. So Galileo told them what they wanted to hear: "Sorry, I take that back."

As a result, his sentence was reduced to life imprisonment. He was seventy years old, and looking more dead than alive. The council of the Inquisition let him go home under house arrest.

Young science students moved in with him, just like old times, and Galileo got back to work. He eventually went completely blind and everything hurt, so his students had to carry him around in a chair, but he kept working. He lived for another seven years.

Eventually, the lead poisoning got to him. Galileo died of kidney failure on January 8, 1642, in Arcetri, Italy. He was seventy-seven years old. He had lived the equivalent of two lifetimes.

Because of the Inquisition, Galileo wasn't allowed to have a fancy funeral. He was buried in a small closet in the Basilica of Santa Croce.

Ninety-five years later, the world of science caught up with Galileo, and his remains were moved to a big marble monument in the church. While they were at it, some fans removed a vertebra, a tooth, and three fingers from Galileo's right hand.

Galileo's middle finger is on display at the Museum of the History of Science in Florence, Italy. Engraved below his middle finger are these words: *This is the finger, belonging to the illustrious hand that ran through the skies, pointing at the immense spaces, and singling out new stars . . .*

It's more likely he pointed at the stars with his pointer finger, saving his middle finger to point at the Inquisition.

The church didn't officially apologize for its treatment of Galileo until 1992—three hundred and fifty years after his death.

63

MISSING FINGERS, VERTEBRA, AND TOOTH

IN 1737, WHILE GALILEO'S BODY was being moved to a larger tomb, fans took three of his fingers, a vertebra, and a tooth.

- One finger is at the Museum of the History of Science, in Florence.
- The vertebra is at the University of Padua, Italy.
- Two fingers and the tooth were kept by an Italian marquis, but they disappeared around 1905. In 2009, two fingers and a tooth were sold at auction without any identification. Turns out they were Galileo's long-lost body parts.

LEAD POISONING

LEAD POISONING CAN CAUSE INTENSE stomach pain and mental disturbances. Causes of lead poisoning:

- lead glazes on plates, bowls, and utensils
- lead-crystal decanters
- wine cured in lead casks
- lead added to wine and other foods as a sweetener and to stop spoilage

THE ROMAN INQUISITION

THE INQUISITION WAS AN EFFORT by the Roman Catholic Church to seek out and punish heretics. A heretic was anyone who opposed the teachings of the church.

In 1231, a special court was created to investigate heretics. In 1542, the Congregation of the Holy Office took control of the Inquisition. The main operations were in France, Germany, Italy, and Spain. The judges were Dominican and Franciscan friars.

The Inquisitors often misused their power, imprisoning, torturing, and burning their victims. For centuries, people lived in fear for their lives.

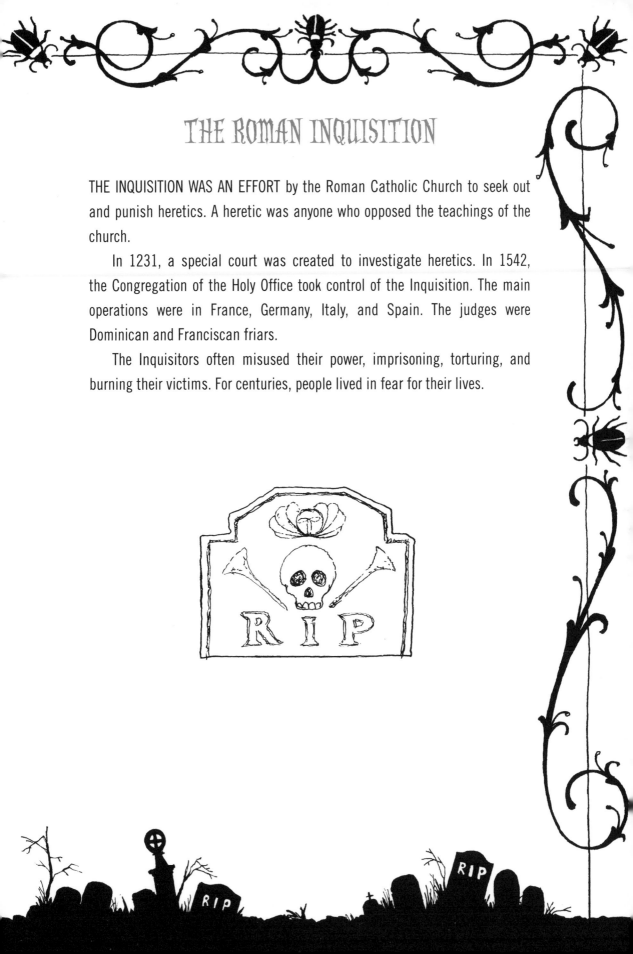

WOLFGANG AMADEUS MOZART

EVERY GOOD BOY DOES FINE

Musician and Composer
Born: Salzburg, Austria,
January 27, 1756
Died: Vienna, Austria,
December 5, 1791
35 years old

WOLFGANG AMADEUS MOZART had a golden ear and magic fingers. As a little kid, he'd hear a piece of music only once and be able to play it back perfectly. People paid through their noses to watch this young genius sit and play the pianoforte before his feet even reached the floor. So Mozart's father took him on a four-year concert tour to perform for the likes of Marie Antoinette and King George III, all before little Wolfie was even ten. Mozart plucked billions of notes out of countless instruments with those talented hands, and when he got sick, his fingers were the first to go.

The boy wonder supported his family in grand style. They bought fancy clothes and a carriage with seven horses and moved to a better

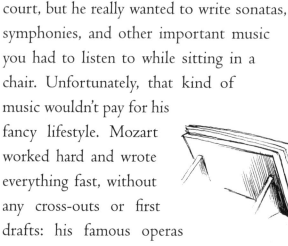

part of town. His father even charged admission to watch him practice. Mozart performed 24/7. But the gigs dried up when Mozart grew into a gawky teen with a huge head. He still cried easily and always loved a good fart joke, but his cute, money-making prodigy years were definitely over. His father was not amused.

Mozart became the concertmaster of the Salzburg court and taught music to the children of nobility, but the pay was low. He moved to Vienna in his twenties, but Emperor Joseph didn't hire him. Mozart made money writing dance songs for the balls at court, but he really wanted to write sonatas, symphonies, and other important music you had to listen to while sitting in a chair. Unfortunately, that kind of music wouldn't pay for his fancy lifestyle. Mozart worked hard and wrote everything fast, without any cross-outs or first drafts: his famous operas

The Magic Flute, The Marriage of Figaro, and *Don Giovanni,* to name a few. But he also partied hard, primped, and shopped till he dropped.

Mozart married Constanze Weber. She came from a musical family and she knew a man with rhythm when she saw one. They had six children, but only two survived to adulthood.

When things got tough, he sold his wife's silver and jewels to make some cash. Mozart could keep a beat, but his forward-thinking innovative music was out of sync with his own times, so he ended up a starving artist.

Throughout his life, he would get a sore throat and then his shoulders, hips, knees, and finger joints swelled up and hurt so badly he couldn't move. Nobody knew what it was.

Bloodsucking slugs called leeches were used to suck out the so-called bad blood from his joints, which is what doctors of the time believed caused illness. The sore joint was shaved and pricked. The leech was kept in a cup until it latched onto the knee or the elbow, and several hours later—after the leech was full of blood—it fell off.

One day, an unknown messenger came with a request for Mozart to write a requiem (death song) for a person whose identity the messenger didn't wish to disclose. The pay was good so Mozart jumped at the commission.

While Mozart worked on the requiem, he grew weaker and weaker. He began to get the creepy feeling he was writing the requiem for himself. When Mozart's skin erupted in red pustules, he said, "I'm being poisoned to death."

The doctor's diagnosis was "severe military fever," which was a catchall phrase for "everything is falling apart." It was said to be caused by excessive passions and eating too many plums and cucumbers. Doctors smeared concoctions of warmed turpentine, wax, powdered Spanish flies, and mustard on his body— which made his skin bubble up and blister. Not a pretty picture.

Mozart's hands swelled up: his music-making fingers turned into ten overstuffed sausages. That's when Mozart got into bed.

Soon he began to vomit, his fever spiked, and his rash got worse. His whole body ballooned and he was unable to sit up. He was slumped over in bed and his crippled fingers were too puffed up even to hold a pen. But he hummed and tapped out the requiem, while a musical assistant wrote down the notes for him.

The stink of rotting human filled the apartment. When Mozart said, "I can taste death in my mouth," someone ran to get the priest. But Mozart never wrote that much church music, so the priest wouldn't come over.

They searched for the doctor and eventually found him at the theater, but he wouldn't leave until the performance was over. He knew Mozart could croak any minute and he didn't want to be there when it happened. He did not want to be known as the doctor who failed to save one of the most brilliant human beings of all time. That could really kill a medical career.

After taking the long way, the doctor finally arrived. He put a cold-water-and-vinegar compress on Mozart's forehead. Mozart shivered, then vomited across the room. Two hours later he was dead. Mozart was right in a way; he *was* writing the requiem for himself. Constanze jumped into Mozart's bed to catch what he had so she could die with him. It didn't work.

He had been sick for only fifteen days. Even in death he was quick.

Mozart's final illness had started with a streptococcal (strep) infection in his throat that migrated into his blood and joints, ultimately leading to kidney failure. He didn't finish the requiem, and he didn't get to finish life as an old man, either.

Mozart died on December 5, 1791, in Vienna, Austria. He was only thirty-five years old. They didn't do an autopsy because his corpse was too smelly. The skin was soft and squishy, not stiff like that of a normal dead person.

After a small gathering at a cathedral, a horse and cart picked up Mozart's coffin and clopped three miles to St. Marx cemetery. Nobody went with it because attending the burial wasn't the custom of the time.

Mozart's body was taken out of the reusable coffin, sewn into a body bag, and covered with quicklime to make it decompose faster. He was buried that night or the next morning, depending on when the five or six other unlucky stiffs were on hand to fill up the common grave alongside Mozart. There was no headstone marking the grave because the emperor forbade them—and that was that. Unless you were royalty or super rich, the law required sack burials as they were cheaper and cleaner, so most people were buried this way.

Constanze didn't go to Mozart's grave for seventeen years (again, people didn't do that back then). When she eventually went there, she couldn't find the grave because the person who buried Mozart was dead, and anyway, every seven years the decomposed bodies in common graves were cleaned out and raked over to prepare for more burials.

Today, strep throat can be cured by taking antibiotics. Unfortunately, Mozart died one hundred and forty years before antibiotics were invented.

LEECHING

A LEECH IS A BLOODSUCKING worm. Leeching is the practice of using leeches to get so-called bad blood out of the body.

STEPS FOR SUCCESSFUL LEECHING:

1. Don't use sick leeches.
2. Soak leeches in beer.
3. Smear blood where you want them to take hold.
4. Put leech in a cup and invert onto the skin.
5. Don't let leeches wander off.
6. Let leech drop off when it wants. If you pull it off, its jaw may get stuck in the skin, which will get infected and bleed profusely.
7. Never use on face or neck because they leave disfiguring scars. You'll end up with a discolored eyelid for life if a leech sucks on it.

RECOMMENDED DOSE:

• 15–20 leeches per adult
• 3–6 for kids age five and under
• 1 per infant, and even that may kill the baby

SOMETIMES UNSTOPPABLE BLEEDING follows a leech bite. This is especially dangerous in children.

OUT WITH THE GARBAGE

- Mozart's widow, Constanze, threw away many of Mozart's unfinished musical compositions.

- Beethoven's secretary threw out 260 of the 400 conversation books Beethoven wrote in to communicate with people.

- George and Martha Washington threw away all their love letters to each other.

- Christopher Columbus's family sold off all his maps and charts.

MARIE ANTOINETTE

I DID NOT DO IT
ON PURPOSE

Queen of France
Born: Vienna, Austria,
November 2, 1755
Died: Paris, France,
October 16, 1793
37 years old

MARIA ANTONIA OF Austria was royalty to the tenth power. On her list of dead relatives were the likes of Roman emperors and Mary, Queen of Scots. She was trained in regal attitude and poise and *not* to have anything on her mind, because all she had to do was look good and have babies. Like her ten sisters, Maria Antonia was predestined to marry royalty in some far-off country to keep the Hapsburg dynasty alive. She was a player in the diplomatic strategy of "don't kill us, we're the in-laws." Maria Antonia ended up with the gig of a lifetime—the queen of France. Her baby-making lineage was what the French wanted . . . until all they wanted was her head.

When she was fourteen, old enough to have babies, Maria Antonia was put in a carriage and carted off to France, where she married the fifteen-year-old king-in-training, Louis XVI. When her carriage arrived at the French border, she got an extreme makeover. Her Austrian things were dumped—including all her clothes, her pug dog, Mops, and even her name—as she was transformed into the French Marie Antoinette.

Louis XVI was no prince charming, but she got to live at Versailles palace with a personal staff of five hundred. The only thing the staff couldn't do for her was make a baby. But Marie Antoinette was the boss of her own body, and she wasn't ready to be a mommy. Instead, she threw big parties, shopped for shoes, gambled, and got ridiculous three-foot-high hairdos. The king did metalwork and hunted, but not for her.

Her mother warned the fifteen-year-old newlywed that she should get pregnant fast because her looks were already going.

Meanwhile, the French people were out of work and starving, and they were starting to hate their queen's guts.

It was seven years and three months before the marriage was consummated. They had four children, but two died in childhood. The French Revolution, which began in 1789, destroyed the monarchy. The next king had been born, but the people didn't want kings anymore. They wanted to be free and equal, and they were killing people left and right to get that freedom.

Marie Antoinette and her family were captured and taken as hostages, which was actually better than being on the streets because the angry mob would have torn them limb from limb. Soon after, in 1793, her husband, King Louis XVI, was beheaded on the guillotine.

The guillotine was the new humane decapitating machine. Before, they used an ax and a block. The designer, Dr. Guillotin, said, "The mechanism falls like lightning; the head flies off; the blood spurts . . ." So much blood spurted, the streets were slippery with it. "You won't even feel the slightest pain," Dr. Guillotin proclaimed. But sometimes a severed head would blink or open its mouth to bite whatever was near.

Marie Antoinette's two remaining children were taken away. She was devastated. She was thrown into prison, even though she was visibly ill. Her hair had turned white. Her joints were swollen and achy. To make matters worse, she fainted a lot and had convulsions. She was also showing signs of cancer of the womb.

Two women jailers felt sorry for her and got her lace, linens, and better food. They brought her flowers, put a ribbon in her hair every day, and gave her mineral water instead of the filthy water of the

Seine. But then the women were arrested for treating Marie Antoinette like she was a queen or something.

The next jailer was all business. When Marie Antoinette asked for knitting needles to make socks for her children, who she knew must be cold wherever they were, the request was denied because the pointy needles might be used as weapons. Instead, she pulled out threads from the fabric on the walls and wove them into garters to hold up stockings.

When she was brought to trial, the courtroom was packed with people jeering. The only thing still queenly about her was her calm poise in front of the murderous crowd. She was put in a chair up on a platform so everybody could watch her in her misery. Her lawyer was given only one day to prepare her case, but it didn't really matter. Her fate had already been decided; Marie Antoinette's death would be the communal violence that was needed to bring everyone together.

Every problem France had ever had was blamed on Marie Antoinette, and she wasn't even French.

On the day of her execution, she wore a white dress, black stockings held in place by her homemade garters, and purple shoes with two-inch heels from the good old days. They cut her hair, tied her hands behind her back, and sat her in an open cart pulled by horses. She was carted around for over an hour to pump the crowd into a frenzy.

78

In those shoes, she climbed the scaffold, calm and in control. Then her head was cut off.

Marie Antoinette died on October 16, 1793, in Paris. She was only thirty-seven years old. Her body and head were taken to a nearby graveyard and tossed on the grass while the grave diggers took their lunch break, giving Madame Tussaud (the famous wax modeler) time to sculpt her face in wax before she was put in the ground.

Her death didn't end anything. It was only the beginning of the Reign of Terror. Twenty to forty thousand people—mostly royalty and wealthy citizens—were killed in the next two years.

By 1815, kings were briefly back in power, and Marie Antoinette's body was dug up. The two hand-sewn garters that she wore at her execution identified her. She was reburied along with her husband in the Basilica of Saint Denis.

There are no descendants of Marie Antoinette. Her son escaped the guillotine but died in prison two years later of tuberculosis at age ten. Her daughter was freed at seventeen and married off but died childless at seventy-two.

Moments before the executioner cut off Marie Antoinette's head, she accidentally stepped on his foot. She looked up at him and said, "I did not do it on purpose." Those were her last words. And that was the story of her life.

THE GUILLOTINE

THE GUILLOTINE IS A DECAPITATING machine, named after its French inventor, Dr. Guillotin.

- First execution: April 25, 1792
- Last execution: September 10, 1977 . . . Aah!
- The average height of the guillotine is 14 feet.
- The metal blade weighs about 88 pounds.
- The blade falls at 21 feet per second.
- A beheading takes 1/50 of a second.
- Removing the head does not kill the brain. It can stay alive for up to thirteen seconds after decapitation, until it dies from lack of oxygen. Consciousness can cease immediately because there is no blood pressure.

MARIE ANTOINETTE'S HAIRDO

MARIE ANTOINETTE WORE THREE-FOOT-TALL headdresses called *poufs.* The frames were built of wire, cloth, gauze, and horsehair and were covered with powder. Elaborate miniature scenes of current events or feelings were depicted in the *poufs.*

Pouf problems:
- *Poufs* were unwashable, providing havens for spiders, mice, and bugs.
- They were itchy and made it hard to dance.
- *Pouf* wearers had to sleep sitting up.
- Carriage roofs weren't tall enough, so the wearer had to squat down on the floor or stick her head out the window.

SOME FAMOUS LAST WORDS

"All my possessions for a moment of time." —Queen Elizabeth I

"A dying man can do nothing easy." —Benjamin Franklin

" 'Tis well." —George Washington

"Thomas Jefferson still survives." —John Adams

"Strike the tent." —Robert E. Lee

"The fog is rising." —Emily Dickinson

"Good-bye . . . if we meet . . ." —Mark Twain

"It is very beautiful over there." —Thomas Edison

"KHAQQ calling Itasca. We must be on you, but cannot see you.
Gas is running low." —Amelia Earhart

"I have a terrific headache." —Franklin Delano Roosevelt

"I'm bored with it all." —Winston Churchill

"This is a house of peace." —Malcolm X

"Drink to me." —Pablo Picasso

GEORGE WASHINGTON

LITTLE MOUTH OF HORRORS

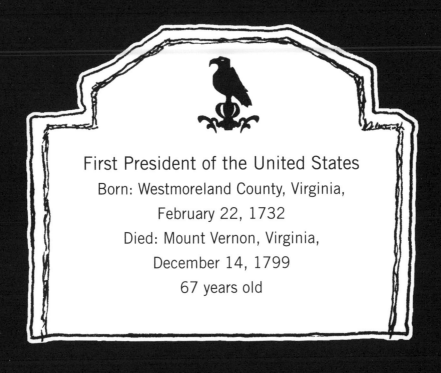

First President of the United States
Born: Westmoreland County, Virginia,
February 22, 1732
Died: Mount Vernon, Virginia,
December 14, 1799
67 years old

CHECK OUT GEORGE Washington's face on the dollar bill. Behind those zippered lips, he didn't have a single tooth in his head. Washington endured decades of pain on a relatively small piece of real estate on his six-foot-three body—the inside of his mouth. Besides his rotten teeth, which had to be pulled out, he had abscesses and carbuncles and other gross-sounding things that had to be lanced, removed, or otherwise severely dealt with. Washington's dentist was anyone with a pair of pliers, and all his dental work was done without any medicine to kill the pain, because it hadn't been invented yet. Washington never complained, but let's just figure it hurt a lot. And, at the end of his life, it was something inside George Washington's mouth that killed him.

Washington was born in Virginia in 1732. Back then, Virginia was still an English colony, but Washington took care of that. As commander in chief of the Continental Army against the British, Washington said bye-bye, thirteen colonies, hello, United States. Washington did such a good job forcing the British to mind their own business that he was elected president of this new country with its three branches of government and freedom of everything. People were fond of him and he could have stayed president as long as he liked, but he thought that would be too much like being a king. Besides, George wanted to go back to being a farmer.

Washington had dentures for most of his life. They are so unbelievably icky that they are on display in a museum. People stare at them and think of Halloween. It was tricky for Washington to do anything with those things tucked into his mouth. He had to eat mashed-up baby food and always laugh with his mouth closed. It doesn't take a brain surgeon to understand why his second inaugural speech was only 135 words long. As for kissing his wife, Martha . . . well, they didn't have any kids. People gave him the benefit of the doubt, though, and he got to be called Father of His Country, anyway.

In 1797, after being president for eight years, Washington finally returned to his farm. But it wasn't long before he had a problem in his mouth.

On the morning of December 14, 1799, Washington woke up boiling hot and gasping for air. Martha and Tobias Lear, his secretary, immediately sent for the doctor—which was harder than it sounds since they were seventy-five years shy of having a phone and a hundred years short of having a car parked out front. Sending for the doctor meant someone had to hop on a horse and gallop over dirt roads to Alexandria, eight miles away, where Dr. Craik lived.

To help Washington breathe, Lear served him a drink of molasses, vinegar, and butter and then wrapped a rag soaked in smelling salts (a stinky chemical) around Washington's neck. It didn't work. He was getting worse by the minute.

Lear got Mr. Rawlins, the overseer, to help. The two of them did what Washington instructed them to do. And it was exactly what everybody expected, too. They took a sharp, double-edged knife, called a bloodletting blade, and cut deep into a vein in Washington's arm so that his blood flowed out into a bowl. They got half a pint of blood out of him.

This was called bloodletting, and it had been performed on sick people for about a gajillion years. Doctors thought bad blood accumulated and stagnated in the body and needed to be removed. Except they overlooked a couple of things. Number one, it was painful, and number two, it made patients feel worse. Nobody seemed to notice those things until the early 1900s, when doctors finally quit doing it.

When Dr. Craik arrived a few hours later, he saw Washington struggling for every breath. Dr. Craik used his advanced medical knowledge to give Washington the blister-beetle treatment. Highly poisonous beetles were ground up and smeared all over George's neck. This made a field of blood blisters across Washington's neck that Dr. Craik then drained.

A couple more doctors showed up and examined the patient. Second and third opinions are always a good idea. Washington was almost dead by then; he couldn't speak and he was drooling profusely. Putting their medical noggins together, they decided to give him a second blistering and another good bleeding.

Hey, thanks for coming.

In 1799, even on a good day, medicine was a crapshoot. Washington had top-of-the-line medical care, but without even a tongue depressor or a thermometer in their bags, it was close to impossible for his doctors to diagnose what was wrong with Washington, much less figure out how to fix him.

So like three blind mice repeatedly banging into the same dead end in a maze, the doctors bled him again and again, draining a total of about 80 ounces of blood out of George Washington. A grown man has only 192 ounces of blood, and taking away Washington's oxygen-carrying blood was a ginormous mistake, considering he had been slowly suffocating since dawn.

86

Washington's doctors tried a couple more remedies from hell. He got a dose of calomel (mercurous chloride) that made him go to the bathroom. Then they gave him tartar emetic, a chemical to make him throw up. With those two treatments, everything inside Washington's stomach made a beeline for the nearest exit. And since there were no bathrooms in 1799, Washington had to emergency poop and puke into bowls right next to his bed.

By the end of the day, Washington was running on empty. He begged, "You had better not take any more trouble about me; but let me go off quietly; I cannot last long."

But they did not let him go. They applied more blister beetles and stuck wheat-bran poultices all over his legs and feet to suck up every last drop of liquid he had left in him.

He died that night, on December 14, 1799. He was sixty-seven years old.

An infection on that small piece of real estate on his large body—the inside of his mouth—killed George Washington. He most likely died of epiglottitis, an infection on the flap of skin at the back of the tongue that protects the windpipe.

Today, a simple dose of antibiotics would have cured him.

BLOODLETTING

BLOODLETTING WAS THE EXTRACTION OF so-called bad blood from the body by using a knife to open a vein.

BLOODLETTING DOS:
- DO use a sharp, clean knife. A dirty knife could cause inflammation and death.
- DO select the largest vein at the bend of the arm.
- DO aim the knife carefully.
- DO place a bowl in the right position to catch the blood.

BLOODLETTING DON'TS:
- DON'T hit a nerve—even though it is almost impossible to avoid them.
- DON'T soak the patient in his own blood. Don't soak the sheets, either.
- DON'T touch the wound with your sweaty fingers because an abscess might develop, followed by the impairment of the entire arm, which will then lead to a hasty death.

DON'T TRY THIS AT HOME!

PRESIDENTIAL DEATH FACTS

THREE OF THE FIRST FIVE U.S. PRESIDENTS DIED ON THE FOURTH OF JULY:
- 2nd president, John Adams: July 4, 1826
- 3rd president, Thomas Jefferson: July 4, 1826
- 5th president, James Monroe: July 4, 1831

DIED WHILE PRESIDENT:

William Henry Harrison • Zachary Taylor • Abraham Lincoln
James A. Garfield • William McKinley • Warren G. Harding
Franklin D. Roosevelt • John F. Kennedy

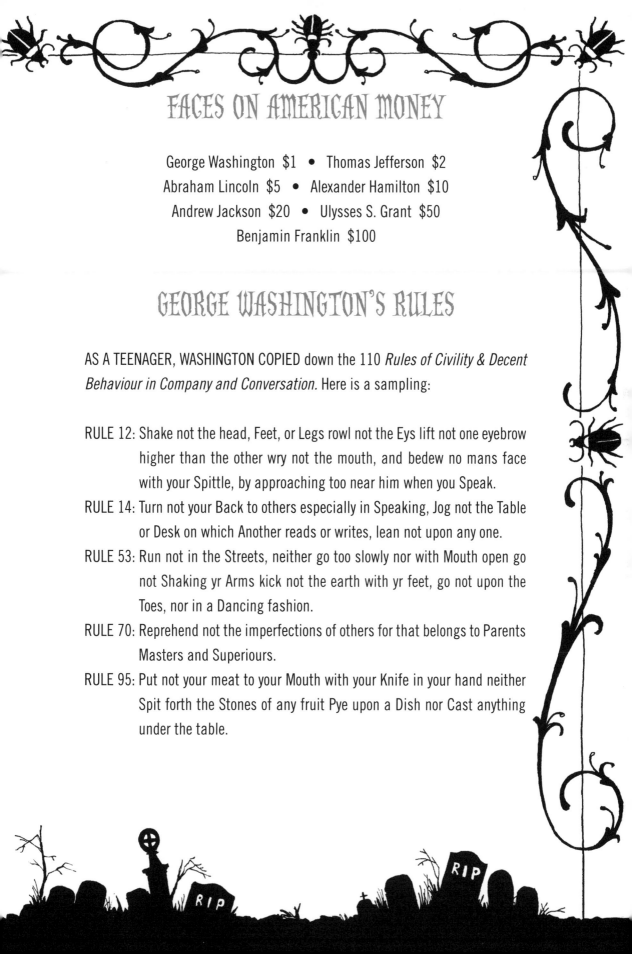

FACES ON AMERICAN MONEY

George Washington $1 • Thomas Jefferson $2
Abraham Lincoln $5 • Alexander Hamilton $10
Andrew Jackson $20 • Ulysses S. Grant $50
Benjamin Franklin $100

GEORGE WASHINGTON'S RULES

AS A TEENAGER, WASHINGTON COPIED down the 110 *Rules of Civility & Decent Behaviour in Company and Conversation.* Here is a sampling:

RULE 12: Shake not the head, Feet, or Legs rowl not the Eys lift not one eyebrow higher than the other wry not the mouth, and bedew no mans face with your Spittle, by approaching too near him when you Speak.

RULE 14: Turn not your Back to others especially in Speaking, Jog not the Table or Desk on which Another reads or writes, lean not upon any one.

RULE 53: Run not in the Streets, neither go too slowly nor with Mouth open go not Shaking yr Arms kick not the earth with yr feet, go not upon the Toes, nor in a Dancing fashion.

RULE 70: Reprehend not the imperfections of others for that belongs to Parents Masters and Superiours.

RULE 95: Put not your meat to your Mouth with your Knife in your hand neither Spit forth the Stones of any fruit Pye upon a Dish nor Cast anything under the table.

I HATE ISLANDS

Emperor of France
Born: Corsica, France,
August 15, 1769
Died: the island of St. Helena,
May 5, 1821
51 years old

NAPOLEON GOT TO be the emperor of France because he wanted to. Nobody else was running France after the French Revolution, so it was his for the taking. It didn't matter that his diplomatic skills were weak; nothing says "I'm in charge" better than setting off a cannonball in your yard.

There are plenty of famous paintings of Napoleon seizing other countries and appearing manly with his hand tucked in his shirt. Turns out, he was just protecting his weakest spot—his stomach. What killed him was growing right under his hand.

Napoleon got into military school at nine years old because his dad knew somebody who knew somebody. Pretty soon, Napoleon had cast-iron resolve about what he'd be when he grew up. And even though he grew up shorter than most and always had something to prove, he was a man on a mission. His map reading and attack-from-behind strategies made him the best player of Capture the Flag in the whole world. He took over Italy, Austria, Prussia

(Germany), and a mess of other places. Napoleon became famous for pillaging, looting, and killing five million friends and foes—and not caring one little bit.

Napoleon was married twice, but he was always off at one battlefield or another. And even when he was home, his heart wasn't in it. His first wife, Josephine, didn't miss him that much, and his second wife, Marie-Louise, who was Marie Antoinette's grandniece, was too busy raising *l'enfant* Napoleon II to care.

Great Britain, Austria, Russia, and Prussia had had enough of Napoleon. They took over Paris and forced Napoleon to give up. He was exiled to the island of Elba. He hated islands: there wasn't much to

92

conquer, and once he did he'd be out of work. Napoleon escaped from the island *tout de suite*. He returned to France and got back in power.

One hundred days later, British and Prussian armies defeated Napoleon at Waterloo, and he was captured again. Exile location number two was another island—St. Helena, a seventy-day sail to a dot in the middle of the southern Atlantic Ocean. But Napoleon wasn't alone. There were five warships and three thousand annoyed English officers stuck there to guard him, many of whom slept with a pencil and paper under their pillow so they could take notes and later write about Napoleon in their memoirs.

After sitting around the island for five years, killing nobody, Napoleon's body grew a deep layer of fat. His body became "feminized." He got soft and curvy. Luckily, artists weren't doing his portrait anymore, because it would have looked like a painting of a pear-shaped old lady. He lost all his hair (except that on his head). The sun gave him a headache, and he needed help standing. Plus, there was a piercing pain in his stomach that never quit.

He had hiccups that went on for days and days. Not the cute kind, but the kind that people try to scare out of a person. It's a good guess Napoleon was hard to scare.

To make him better, doctors used chemical warfare on the lining of Napoleon's stomach. This triggered vomiting on a massive scale. They also mixed together a manly dose of a highly explosive ingredient known to detonate an intestinal bomb with 100 percent accuracy. The resulting poop gave new meaning to the phrase "surprise attack from behind." Unfortunately for everyone, Napoleon did you-know-what right in the bed, every couple of hours, for the next few days. It was said to be "impressive."

While the doctors took a break, Napoleon's *valet de chambre* worked nonstop changing the sheets—and sneaking moments to write about the experience.

Napoleon got worse. Then the doctors actually blistered his thighs and stomach, trying to release what was killing him. This was followed by a soothing smear of wax, resin, and mutton suet. Flies were attracted to all the interesting things going on around Napoleon, and swatting flies off Napoleon was one more task for the busy valet until the patient was put under a net.

On his last day, Napoleon was laughing crazily and throwing up black stuff. So the doctors blistered his feet, his chest, and one calf. His eyes opened and then rolled back in his head. *C'est fini.* Napoleon was dead. He died on May 5, 1821. He was fifty-one years old.

His body was washed with *eau de cologne* and laid out on his old army cot.

Word hit the street quickly on the island: "We're going home!" And three thousand soldiers started packing.

The next morning, a famous sketch was drawn of Napoleon's dead body. Napoleon's valet did a drawing, too, but he put himself in the foreground faking grief. That was right before he took some Napoleonic goodies he felt he deserved: a glass and a pen.

The doctors did an autopsy. The chest was opened. *Quelle surprise!* There was a heart. It was cut out and put into a jar. Then they found what had killed him: a cancerous stomach ulcer. It was in the spot

94

where Napoleon had his hand in so many paintings. Finally, the dead body was sewn back together. Napoleon's valet took the bloody autopsy sheet and cut it up for souvenirs. The valet also cut off all Napoleon's hair to put in frames and lockets.

After a big ceremony and a gun salute, Napoleon was put in the ground under some trees. Their branches were stripped for souvenirs. The three thousand officers were in the streets, not paying their respects but getting in line to catch the first boat out of there. The valet went home with three lead-sealed trunks.

Nineteen years after Napoleon died, the British allowed Napoleon's remains to be returned to France. First they took a quick peek inside Napoleon's coffin to make sure he was still dead. Then they took his corpse back to Paris, where he now lies in Napoleon's Tomb, an ornate place for a hero—except he wasn't one.

Napoleon had wanted his heart sent to his wife. But as in life, she never received it.

FIRST AMBULANCE

BARON DOMINIQUE-JEAN LARREY, A PRIVATE surgeon to Napoleon, created the first ambulance for the wounded men on the battlefield in 1792. Even with battlefield ambulances, 500,000 of his own men (one-sixth of the French population) were killed in the Napoleonic Wars.

The first motorized ambulance was invented in 1895 and used by the French Army Corps in 1900.

NAPOLEON COMPLEX

A "NAPOLEON COMPLEX" DESCRIBES PEOPLE who think they have a shortcoming and try to cover it up by overdoing other things in their lives. They say Napoleon's crazy desire to take over the world was to compensate for being short. Napoleon was average in height for the times (five feet five); he just seemed short because he hung around his Imperial Guards, who were extra tall.

ST. HELENA

- 1,750 miles from South Africa
- 1,800 miles from South America
- 4,000 miles from England
- 700 miles from the closest island, Ascension Island
- As in Napoleon's time, the only way to get to St. Helena is by ship

BOOKS ABOUT NAPOLEON

ACCORDING TO HISTORIAN PAUL JOHNSON, there are more books written about Napoleon than about any other person except Jesus Christ. For example, twelve people in Napoleon's inner circle on St. Helena wrote books about him: three doctors, three valets, three army men, one female friend, one local official, and one teenage girl.

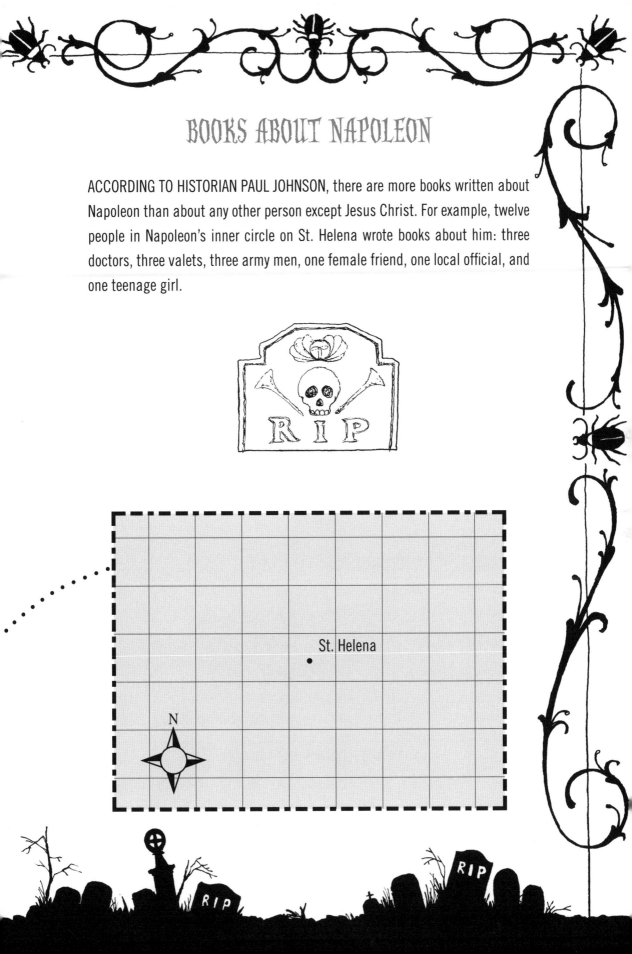

LUDWIG VAN BEETHOVEN

BETWEEN THOSE EARS

Musician and Composer
Born: Bonn, Germany,
December 17, 1770
Died: Vienna, Austria,
March 26, 1827
56 years old

BEETHOVEN'S DAD FORCED him to practice the piano, as dads have done since the dawn of music. We don't know what tunes Beethoven practiced, but today kids are forced to play "Für Elise" and "Moonlight Sonata," melodies that Beethoven wrote. Practice paid off for Beethoven and he became a musical genius. He played his first gig when he was eight years old. He performed for kings, did concert tours, had a lot of fans, and even had long hair like a rock star. And Beethoven's hair, it turns out, helped uncover how he died.

Today, you can get Beethoven's music as a ringtone on your cell phone. But back then, without CDs or iPods, the only way to hear his music was live. You had to be there with him in concert. However, something went wrong for Beethoven. Eventually Beethoven couldn't hear what he was playing at his own concerts because he went deaf.

He started losing his hearing when he was twenty-seven. By forty-five, he was totally deaf. Over time, Beethoven had to imagine the music he was playing. He only heard what he composed *inside* his head, *between* his ears, *under* his long hair. When he wrote his ninth symphony, he couldn't hear a thing. That's like Leonardo da Vinci painting *Mona Lisa* with his eyes closed.

Even though he was unable to hear, he always composed at his piano. He picked up and moved with his piano forty times during his life, and that was no

easy thing, considering there were no trucks or cranes or piano dollies.

Being deaf made him not want to be with people, especially ladies. He was a bachelor and there weren't any little Beethovens, so it's kind of funny and sad that he was named the greatest Romantic composer.

There was no sign language back then, so Beethoven and his friends wrote notes back and forth, like texting but with pencil and paper.

Beethoven was clumsy and cranky most of the time. He had stomach problems that made him feel lousy for the last thirty years of his life, with constant diarrhea, vomiting, and gas. Houses had no plumbing yet, which means there was no toilet, either. He had to use a thing called a chamber pot.

In 1827, Beethoven got pneumonia and couldn't shake it. His stomach was killing him. He couldn't go to the bathroom (chamber pot), his skin was the color of a banana, and blood dripped out of his mouth. Then he got dropsy. That's when fluid inside your body that's supposed to get out can't. Very quickly, Beethoven's body filled up with rotting fluid. He got huge. His stomach bloated and the skin stretched across it as tight as a balloon.

A doctor in 1827 didn't know much more than a doctor in the Middle Ages, so Beethoven's doctors figured all that Beethoven needed was a drain to get the liquid out. They took him to the hospital. But back then, half the people who went into the hospital came out dead.

At the hospital a hole was drilled into Beethoven's stomach, and then they stuck a hose in it. Beethoven probably experienced the most painful day of his entire life. Awake and without pain medicine,

Beethoven watched forty cups of grayish brown puslike gunk flow out of his belly—enough to fill ten quart bottles. This was before stitches, so his doctor plugged the hole with some rags and sent Beethoven home.

The gunk continued to leak out of the hole in Beethoven's stomach. But his belly got even bigger than it had been before they took him to the hospital. During the next few weeks he went back to the hospital three more times to have his stomach drained. His doctor reinserted the hose into the same hole each time. And, no surprise, the hole got infected.

So his doctors attempted another "cure." They tried to sweat out the liquid with a steam bath. They propped Beethoven up in a tub filled with jugs of hot water. A sheet was spread on top of the tub. They didn't cover Beethoven's head—they were smart enough not to mess with the part where all the music came from. After a few hours, the sheet was removed. Instead of sweating out the liquid, his body had absorbed the steam like a giant sponge. Poor Beethoven was as big as the Goodyear Blimp.

Since there were no such things as photographs to remember him by, a friend summoned an artist to make a drawing of Beethoven shortly before he slipped into unconsciousness.

On March 26, 1827, Beethoven died. He was fifty-six years old.

After he died, souvenir hunters took snips of his hair. Some got snips when nobody was looking, some paid for snips, and some had already snipped his hair before he was officially dead. By the end of the day, he was completely bald. Keeping locks of hair as mementos was a quirky custom, but a common one before photography.

The doctors cut Beethoven's body open and performed an autopsy. All his inside parts were too small or too big, too soft or too hard— the opposite of what they should have been. The autopsy folks sliced Beethoven's skull crosswise at the top; they wanted to look inside his famous head to see if they could detect what made him so special. They took out his temporal bones to study them. But, mysteriously, the bones disappeared, and a little while later the autopsy reports disappeared, too.

To remember what he looked like, wet plaster was smashed into the contours of Beethoven's face to make a thing called a death mask. It was unpleasant and hard to do because, from the eyebrows up, the top of Beethoven's skull had been sawed through at the autopsy the day before.

Twenty thousand fans came to his funeral. A ring of white roses was placed on his head to hide the mess they had made at the autopsy.

The grave digger was offered a lot of money to remove what was left of Beethoven's head before the burial and drop it at a secret location. But the grave digger said no. A night watchman was hired so that no one would dig up Beethoven and take his head.

103

Thirty-six years later, in 1863, Beethoven's music was even more popular. His body was dug up and put in a better coffin. The experts took another look at his famous head. His skull was measured and cast in plaster. By then, photography had been invented, so they took some pictures of it, too. To make sure no one stole Beethoven's skull while it was being studied, an old friend took it home and slept with it next to his bed. But, mysteriously, some of the photographs of Beethoven's skull disappeared.

Twenty-five years later, in 1888, Beethoven's music was even more popular. They dug him up again and put him in an even bigger, nicer cemetery. It was then that they noticed ten skull pieces were missing. Turns out the friend who took Beethoven's skull home in 1863 to keep it safe probably ended up giving pieces of it away: some way, somehow, a skull collector now had the fragments of Beethoven's skull.

The family of the skull collector passed the fragments from generation to generation. It wasn't until 1990 that the person who last inherited the bones wanted to get rid of them. Beethoven scholars couldn't wait to get their hands on them.

In 1994, a lock of Beethoven's hair turned up at auction and sold for $7,300.

Scientists analyzed the lock of hair and figured out something about Beethoven they never could have guessed

ITEM 12
BIG B'S HAIR

when he was alive in the 1800s. Poor Beethoven had massive lead poisoning—one hundred times the normal level. In 2010, his skull fragments were analyzed. One piece had a high level of lead, but the other didn't. They're not sure how he might have gotten lead poisoning, but it could have caused every problem he had with his stomach, along with his clumsiness and irritability. But it did not cause his deafness.

Stay tuned. Beethoven is more famous now than ever. Who knows what else will turn up?

OTHER ROMANTIC~ERA COMPOSERS

Berlioz

Bizet

Brahms

Chopin

Dvořák

Liszt

Mendelssohn

Schubert

Tchaikovsky

SIGN LANGUAGE

GIACOBBO PEREIRE OF SPAIN IS one of the inventors of a formal sign language. Pereire's wife was deaf and in 1749 he devoted himself to finding a language for her. Unfortunately, Beethoven didn't know sign language, nor did his family or friends.

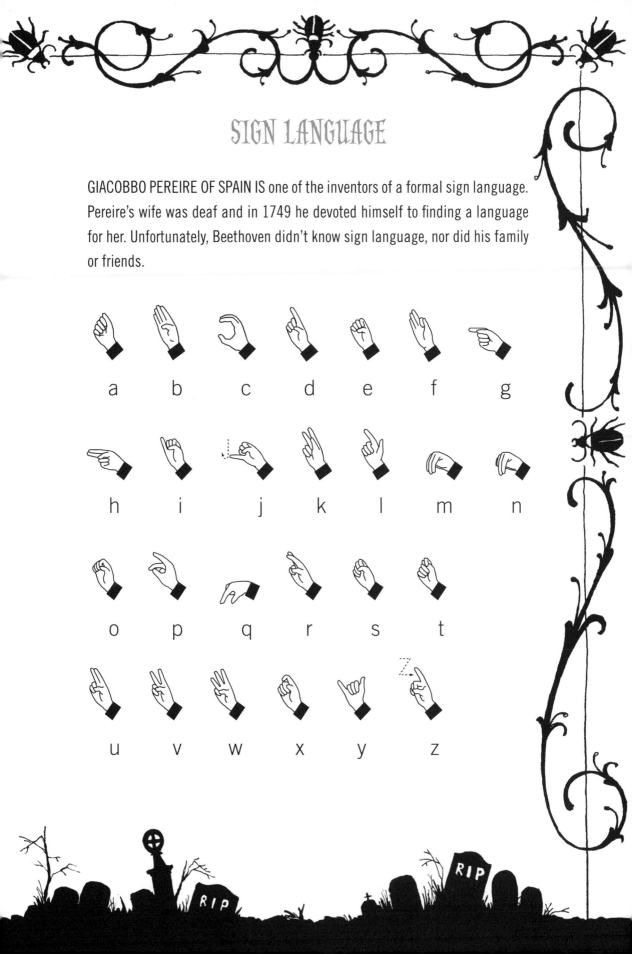

EDGAR ALLAN POE

OH, WOE IS POE

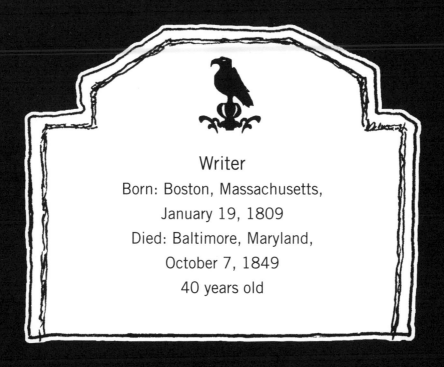

Writer
Born: Boston, Massachusetts,
January 19, 1809
Died: Baltimore, Maryland,
October 7, 1849
40 years old

POE ATTENDED A lot of funerals. When he wasn't going to funerals, he wrote stories about dead people (or soon-to-be-dead people) living in torture chambers, haunted houses, and other creepy locales with zero chance of escape, like in "The Pit and the Pendulum," "The Fall of the House of Usher," and "The Murders in the Rue Morgue." His stories start out with lines like "I was sick—sick unto death with that long agony," and that's the cheery part. Misery, loneliness, and death are the grim themes of his work . . . and of his life. Lots of bad stuff happened to him, and then he died.

Poe's major woe started when his dad split, leaving Poe's ailing mother and three small children on their own. By the time Poe was three, his mom had died of tuberculosis. He watched her cough up blood and waste away. Little Poe sat in a room with his mom's dead body for a few days until it was taken away and buried. After that, he slept with the covers over his head because he thought a dead person would come get him in the middle of the night.

Abandoned and orphaned, Poe was separated from his brother and sister and raised by foster parents, Fanny and John Allan. Fanny loved Poe, but John hated his guts. Poe grew to have a large forehead, a brooding stare, and a gift for words. When Poe was fifteen, his first girlfriend dropped dead of tuberculosis just like his mother. By the time he was twenty, he'd gone to college, dropped out, joined the army, dropped out, and published his first book of poems; writing became his life's work.

Then stepmom Fanny started coughing up blood and she died of tuberculosis. John told Poe to get lost.

Poe reconnected with his older brother, Henry, but then Henry died of tuberculosis. Poe moved in with an aunt and his first cousin Virginia. He fell in love with Virginia and they got married (acceptable in those days), but then, guess what? Virginia died of tuberculosis.

There is no denying it: Poe was a disaster magnet.

Poe used his bad case of the gloomies when he put pen to paper. In 1845, his poem "The Raven" was published in the *Evening Mirror*, and it became an instant classic. It turned Poe into a celebrity and everybody wanted to know him, but it didn't pay the bills and he was

110

starving most of the time. He was paid practically nothing and, because there were no copyright laws, what he wrote could be freely copied by others. In his whole life he earned only three hundred dollars for all his writing. Reduced to begging people for help, sometimes he'd send letters to far-off relatives and acquaintances to ask for money.

Despite these troubles, Poe miraculously kept writing. But there was another problem: he tried to ditch his troubles by drinking. People expected that when he walked into a room he would probably be drunk. Or he'd wander the streets missing a shoe, disheveled and "disoriented" (a polite word used at the time for "drunk"). Though he tried many times, Poe couldn't keep a paying job. He pursued a couple of wealthy women in the hope of finding love and security, but being a drunk is not that attractive. People avoided him like the plague.

"My life seems wasted—the future looks a dreary blank," Poe wrote to his aunt.

Desperate, he left Richmond, Virginia, to head to New York City on a wild goose chase in pursuit of work. Poe's first stop was Baltimore, where he accidentally walked off with someone else's cane and lost his luggage.

And then, for the next six days, Poe completely vanished. There is no record of where he was or what he was doing and, for a relatively famous man, that was hard to do unless he was drunk, facedown somewhere—which was very possible.

On election day, Poe showed up at a bar called Ryan's 4th Ward Polls in Baltimore, so named because it was used as an election-polling place. He was a wreck. He was disoriented (see previous page). His vest and neck cloth (like a tie, only wider and tied differently) were gone, and he was wearing someone else's filthy clothes inside out and backward.

It was a complete coincidence that two of Poe's distant relatives came into the bar. They didn't have any fond family memories; Poe had been drunk and belligerent the last time they saw him, and it looked like he was at it again. They dragged his limp body out of there and dropped him at the hospital so he could sleep it off in the drunk ward.

At the hospital the next day, Poe was jumpy and agitated. He was talking, but it was all gibberish. The doctors assumed he was still drunk.

Overnight he became less erratic, but the next morning he still wasn't making sense. He should have sobered up by then. The doctors offered Poe water to drink, but he wouldn't take it.

Poe woke up the next morning delirious and began calling out the name "Reynolds." He blathered about Reynolds until three the following morning.

Then Edgar Allan Poe died. It was October 7, 1849, and he was only forty years old. The cause of death was given as "congestion of the brain," which was a common medical phrase at the time that explained practically nothing.

Over the years everybody assumed that Poe had died of alcohol poisoning. But how could he still have been drunk after not drinking a drop for four days in the hospital?

Recently, doctors reexamined Poe's medical records. It's possible a rabid animal bit him. He refused to drink water at the hospital; people with rabies are unable to swallow water. And people with

rabies also act like they're, well . . . drunk—which would explain why he didn't sober up.

The penniless Poe might have been part of a voter-fraud scheme right before he died. Potential voters at the time were kept in rooms where they would change into various clothes and then go to different polling places so they could vote more than once. The payoff was free alcohol. And "Reynolds"—the name Poe kept calling out at the end—was the name of a polling official.

To this day, no one is completely certain if Poe died of rabies or of something else, but one thing seems clear: Poe wanted to take his place in the realm of the dead in a big hurry. After all, everybody he had ever loved was already there.

TUBERCULOSIS

MORE THAN A BILLION PEOPLE have died of tuberculosis. It is the biggest killer of all time. One of every seven people died from tuberculosis in the 1800s, when Poe was alive.

A person catches tuberculosis by breathing in airborne bacteria when a sick person sneezes or coughs. It used to be called "consumption" because it seemed to consume its victims. The symptoms are coughing up blood, wasting away, fever, and chest pain. Cattle, frogs, turtles, some birds, and even fish can get tuberculosis.

The first tuberculosis vaccine was developed in 1921. Today, tuberculosis can be cured with antibiotics, but it still kills almost two million people every year.

RABIES

PEOPLE GET RABIES WHEN AN animal infected with rabies—most likely a dog, cat, skunk, cow, wolf, or raccoon—bites them. You can also get rabies from breathing the air in caves where infected bats live.

In most cases, symptoms appear one to three months after exposure, depending on when the virus reaches the brain. Symptoms include restlessness, confusion, agitation, terror, and an inability to swallow water.

Louis Pasteur developed a vaccine against rabies in 1885. Fifty-five thousand people still die of rabies every year, mostly in Asia and Africa.

FIRST DETECTIVE STORY

Poe's story "The Murders in the Rue Morgue" was published in *Graham's Magazine* in 1841. It is considered the first detective story ever written. The detective's name is C. Auguste Dupin.

CHARLES DICKENS

A TALE OF TWO BRAINS

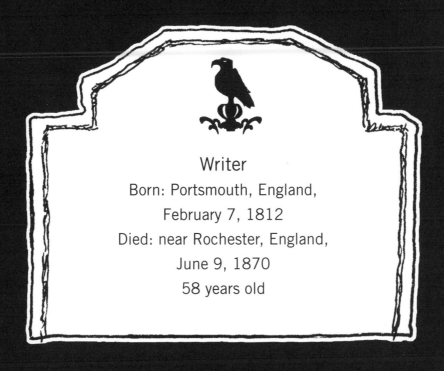

Writer
Born: Portsmouth, England,
February 7, 1812
Died: near Rochester, England,
June 9, 1870
58 years old

IT WAS THE best of times for Charles Dickens, the richest, most famous author in the 1800s. But it was the worst of times for anyone who knew him. Dickens was incredibly talented, but he was also a moody, dirt-phobic control freak. People described him as a "human hurricane." He explained sitting down to work as "writing my head off." Dickens felt like his head was coming off because he had a torrential chemical imbalance going on beneath his comb-over. It fueled his art, but it ruined every relationship he had. It wasn't his fault, and it's not what killed him. Blood-flow logjams in his brain ultimately left him as dead as a doornail.

At twelve years old, Dickens had a full-time job pasting labels on jars. By seventeen, he was a court reporter writing in shorthand. After he quit that job and became a real writer, though, the word "short" never described anything Dickens wrote.

Dickens walked ten to twenty miles every day before he sat down to write anything. Without spell-check or a delete button, it was tough being a writer back then. Dickens had to stop to dip a goose-feather quill into a jar of ink every couple of sentences, but nothing stopped him from writing a lot and very fast. He published his first story at twenty-one, and by the time he was twenty-five he was a successful and admired author.

Ebenezer Scrooge from the novel *A Christmas Carol* is his most famous character. Scrooge is a mean, stingy person who doesn't like children. Dickens didn't have to do much research to get Scrooge just right.

Dickens never said anything nice about his wife, Catherine. He considered his ten children to be disappointing, expensive, and messy. If a chair was out of place during his daily inspection of their rooms, the wrath of Daddy Dickens was wacko. The kids were scared whenever he was around. Dickens gave them nicknames like Flaster Floby and Chickenstalker. The kids' nicknames for Dad could have been Shutyourwordhole or Getoveryourself.

But Dickens never got over himself. He burned twenty years' worth of letters he'd received, especially the ones about forcing his wife to leave their house and refusing to let the kids see her family ever again, because he thought only his side of any story was important. And as if he didn't already have enough dominance over everybody, he learned how to hypnotize people.

When he got older, Dickens traveled all over England and America by train, dramatizing his stories in theaters and playing all the characters himself. On performance days, he'd drink rum for breakfast, sherry and champagne for lunch, and then more alcohol for dinner. With all that liquor to drink, who couldn't play all the characters?

But Dickens was having trouble just playing himself.

Sometimes he would collapse onto his left side in excruciating pain. He had kidney stones (crystallized urine) that inched their way through his urinary tract and were about as painful to pass as giving birth to a ball of barbed wire. The prescription of the time was to hop on a horse and shake them loose or, if that didn't work, to drink a broth made from boiling baby animals.

Other times, Dickens's left arm wouldn't go where he wanted it to, and it hurt so much he had to wear it in a sling. Then there were times when he could see only the right side of a room or words on the right side of a piece of paper, but not the left. Still other times Dickens walked in circles when he wanted to walk straight.

Dickens's doctor did a blood-removal treatment called cupping to try to get him to quit circling around. The doctor used a tool called a scarificator, with spring-loaded

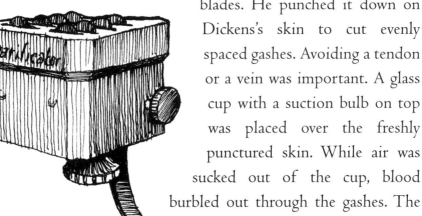

blades. He punched it down on Dickens's skin to cut evenly spaced gashes. Avoiding a tendon or a vein was important. A glass cup with a suction bulb on top was placed over the freshly punctured skin. While air was sucked out of the cup, blood burbled out through the gashes. The doctor scooped up the blood and then made new crosswise cuts on the same spot to get even more blood. A cupping session left a field of bright red welts that lasted weeks.

Things got worse when Dickens had paralysis of the motor functions in his left leg. After a while, the big toe on his lame leg got huge. It was gout, an excruciatingly painful disease people get from living too large on rich food and alcohol. The pain of gout feels something like a shark taking a bite out of your toe.

But Dickens's doctors thought all his problems were caused by too many bumpy train rides. They told him to stop performing, and his manager shortened the engagement tour. But no one got away with

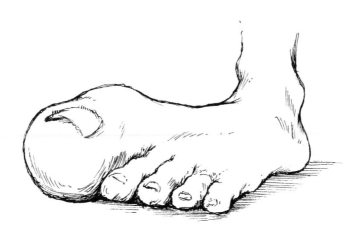

telling Dickens what to do; he told off his manager, throwing a raging fit that no one ever forgot.

Even though he was partially paralyzed, walking in circles, and unable to see half of what he was looking at, Dickens was still able to write, no problem.

That's because different parts of the brain do different things. If the left side of the body isn't working, it's the right side of the brain that's got a problem. The part of Dickens's brain that made up stories was working just fine. He never had creative paralysis.

Still touring, Dickens would show off, bow, wait for more applause, and limp offstage and collapse. Now he kept a doctor (whom he didn't listen to) in the wings at every show. When he forgot how to say *Pickwick Papers*, the name of his first book, his doctor finally told him to go home.

When Dickens returned, the house was all but empty. One unmarried daughter still lived at home, but the rest had already left. His wife had moved away fifteen years before—not that he cared.

His wife's sister had stayed behind, though—most likely because she was on his payroll.

One night at dinner, Dickens jibber-jabbered a bunch of words that didn't fit together; his word magic was gone. Then he fell to the floor. The other part of his brain was shutting down. He was cold and didn't budge all night. The doctors came and tried to warm him up with hot bricks.

Charles Dickens died that night, June 9, 1870. He was fifty-eight years old.

Dickens's "human hurricane" personality would now be diagnosed as manic-depressive illness. It's a disorder that never gets better on its own. With the proper medication, it is manageable today for millions of people.

His doctors didn't understand it at the time, but his left side didn't work because he had had what is known today as a stroke. Dickens had many strokes. Uncontrollable bleeding in Dickens's brain is what killed him.

He made a lovely corpse. So lovely, the artist Sir John Everett Millais came to do a deathbed drawing of him. Before he could begin, he needed to tie Dickens's mouth shut. Maybe Dickens had one more story to tell. Or one more person to tell off.

MANIC-DEPRESSIVE ILLNESS

MANIC-DEPRESSIVE ILLNESS, ALSO KNOWN as bipolar disorder, causes severe shifts in mood, from one emotional extreme to another, and can result in damaged relationships and poor job and school performance.

Manic symptoms: overly happy, wired, impulsive, extreme irritability, moody, unrealistic belief in one's abilities

Depressive symptoms: feeling worried or empty, no interest in anything, tired, depressed

Biopolar disorder lasts a lifetime and there is no cure. Medication helps most people gain control of their intense mood swings, and of their lives.

CUPPING

CUPPING WAS ONE OF THE procedures used to get so-called bad blood out of the body. It was more painful than bleeding or leeching. The skin had to be free of hair and bony prominences, otherwise sufficient sucking action wouldn't be possible. Cupping too close to a blood vessel, nerve, or tendon would hurt a lot and bleed too much. A cup with a suction bulb on top worked best.

Cupping was perfectly safe . . . although sometimes it was followed by annoying if not fatal bleeding.

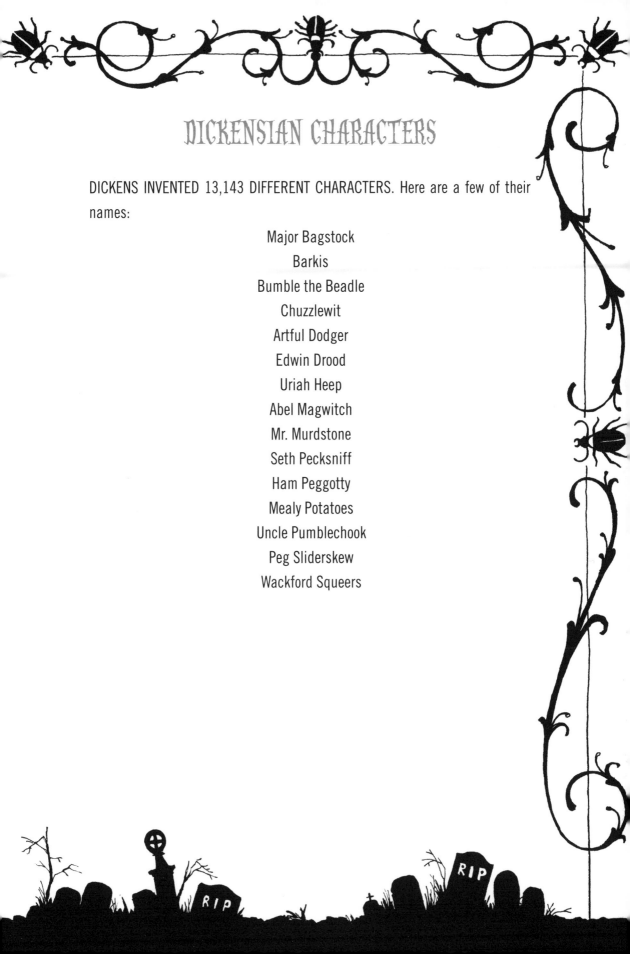

DICKENSIAN CHARACTERS

DICKENS INVENTED 13,143 DIFFERENT CHARACTERS. Here are a few of their names:

Major Bagstock

Barkis

Bumble the Beadle

Chuzzlewit

Artful Dodger

Edwin Drood

Uriah Heep

Abel Magwitch

Mr. Murdstone

Seth Pecksniff

Ham Peggotty

Mealy Potatoes

Uncle Pumblechook

Peg Sliderskew

Wackford Squeers

JAMES A. GARFIELD

JAMES WHO?

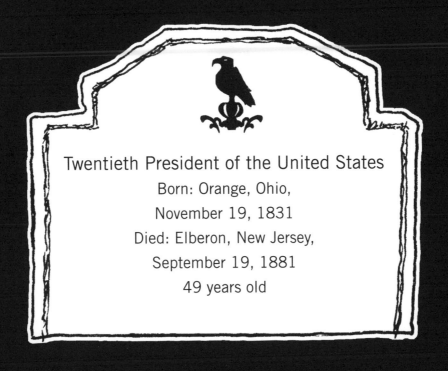

Twentieth President of the United States
Born: Orange, Ohio,
November 19, 1831
Died: Elberon, New Jersey,
September 19, 1881
49 years old

SO **WHO THE** heck was President James Garfield? He's barely mentioned in history books, we don't celebrate his birthday, and there's no money with his face on it. The few schools named Garfield are not named after the famous cartoon cat but after this guy. Garfield was the twentieth president of the United States for only four months before some nut job shot him. And it was easy, too, because Garfield had no bodyguards. Abraham Lincoln had been assassinated sixteen years before, and still nobody thought the president needed protection.

Today, a president can't go anywhere without Secret Service protection, but not back then. Garfield was a sitting duck for anyone with a chip on his shoulder and a screw loose.

In 1881, outlaws like Jesse James and Billy the Kid were holding up trains and shooting people. Local law was enforced with gunfights in the center of town, and a boy of fifteen could join a posse to hunt down a suspected criminal. Almost a quarter of all U.S. currency was counterfeit. The Secret Service had been created by the Treasury to protect the money—but not people. Policemen protected the White House and its grounds—but not the president. Anybody could walk into the White House, and if the president wasn't there, no problem. You could find out when he would be back: his schedule was printed in the daily newspapers.

On July 2, 1881, President Garfield and his secretary of state, James G. Blaine, went to the train station. Charles J. Guiteau, a crazy guy with a gun (who apparently read the daily newspapers), was waiting there. Because no one protected the president, Guiteau was able to walk right behind Garfield and shoot him twice with his snub-nosed .44-caliber British Bulldog revolver. One bullet nicked Garfield's arm and the other hit him in the back. Garfield went down.

Dialing 911 in an emergency was about ninety years down the road and, considering that there were only a couple of phones in Washington at the time—one at the White House and one at the Treasury—calling for help meant Mr. Blaine screaming at the top of his lungs.

Garfield was bleeding all over the place, but he was still alive. A

128

mattress was dragged over for him to lie on, and a woman cradled his head in her lap. A doctor arrived and gave Garfield a shot of brandy to lessen the pain when he examined the bullet hole by sticking his finger in it. Without X-rays, which weren't discovered for another fourteen years, sticking a finger in the bullet hole was the only way to find a bullet. And Garfield's doctor didn't wash his hands or wear gloves.

Pretty soon ten doctors were at the station taking turns poking their unwashed fingers into the hole in Garfield's back. The bullet was inside Garfield's body, but not one of them could find it.

Bullet probes were jammed into the bullet hole to try to dig out the slug. After several tries and plenty of wrong turns, the doctors had missed the bullet path completely and reamed a whole new twelve-inch-long path in Garfield's back. They still couldn't find the bullet. But by then, millions of microscopic germs had been deposited inside Garfield's body.

Since there were no trauma centers at hospitals back then, Garfield was taken in a horse-drawn ambulance to the White House. He was given a glass of champagne and a shot of morphine for the pain. He wasn't expected to live through the night.

Garfield's legs went numb, he vomited every thirty minutes, and the bed got soaked with blood, but he was still alive the next morning.

And that was Day One in what became an eighty-day hunt for the lead bullet in Garfield's back.

The White House was swamped with letters about how to find the bullet—people suggested hanging him up by his feet so the bullet could fall out or sucking it out with a pump. Alexander Graham Bell, the inventor of the telephone, made a contraption that would send a noise through his telephone receiver when it passed over the metal bullet. But Bell didn't realize that Garfield was lying on top of another recent invention—a metal-coil-spring mattress—so over and over Bell's device gave a false reading.

Dear Sir,
To Remove bullet...
① Place president in bucket
② Wave a chicken over his head
③ repeat out loud "OUT BULLET OUT"

A screen was set up around Garfield's bed. For unknown reasons, instead of experienced medical nurses, the wives of cabinet members rotated on a twenty-four-hour schedule, attending to Garfield's needs. His doctors restricted visitors, including the vice president and Garfield's own family.

It wasn't long before the bullet hole got infected. Doctors thought pus was a sign of healing, not infection. Garfield's doctors cut into his wound to make the opening larger so that twice a day they could stick in a rubber hose and drain out the pus. Besides pus, they dug out fabric from his shirt and pieces of his rib.

Weeks went by and there was still no bullet, and Garfield was wasting away. He had high fevers, he threw up everything he ate, and he was delirious. Forty-four days into Garfield's ordeal, his doctors decided not to give him any more food to eat. They only gave him food rectally. The enemas were made of eggs, beef extract, and whiskey. His doctors were starving him to death.

Garfield's whole body became infected. His position was adjusted a hundred times a day so he wouldn't lean on any one spot too long. An infected parotid gland by his right ear made his eye and cheek so swollen, the whole side of his face was paralyzed.

Garfield asked to be taken to the New Jersey shore. In order to make the trip as easy as possible for him, 3,200 feet of train tracks were added so the train could travel right up to the door of the beach house. On the journey there, Garfield's train unexpectedly stopped a few hundred yards shy of the house. People nearby gathered behind the train car and pushed it the rest of the way to his front door.

Two weeks later, on September 19, 1881, less than three months after Garfield was shot, he died. Unfortunately, the infected wound, blood poisoning, and a heart attack did him in. He had lost one hundred pounds in three months.

The autopsy showed that the bullet was nowhere near where his doctors thought it was. The bullet never touched any vital organs. Garfield would have lived if the doctors had kept their dirty hands off him.

Twenty years later, in 1901, President McKinley was assassinated. There was still no Secret Service to protect the president.

Many years after the assassinations of presidents Lincoln, Garfield, and McKinley, Congress legalized the use of federal funds "for the protection of the person of President of the United States." In 1907, two agents were officially assigned full-time to protect President Theodore Roosevelt. Today, there are approximately 3,200 special agents assigned to protect the president, vice president, and their families; former presidents; and visiting heads of foreign states; among several others.

ROBERT TODD LINCOLN

FOUR AMERICAN PRESIDENTS HAVE BEEN assassinated; Abraham Lincoln's son Robert Todd Lincoln was near three of the incidents.

In 1865, President Abraham Lincoln was shot at Ford's Theatre. Robert rushed to the theater and was at his father's bedside when he died.

In 1881, President James A. Garfield was shot in a Washington DC train station. Robert was the secretary of war at the time and was accompanying the president on his trip. Robert rushed to Garfield's side after he was shot.

In 1901, President William McKinley was shot at the Pan-American Exposition in Buffalo, New York. Robert had been invited to join the president in Buffalo, and he happened to arrive just after the president was shot.

SECRET SERVICE TIMELINE

1865
First created to fight counterfeiters

1894
Informal protection of President Cleveland

1902
Assumed full protection of President Theodore Roosevelt (approved by Congress in 1907)

1908
Protection of the president-elect

MEDICAL ADVANCES TOO LATE FOR GARFIELD

Antisepsis: 1865 (Garfield's doctors didn't try to stop the spread of germs through cleanliness; the practice wasn't widely adopted until the late 1880s)

Rubber gloves: 1890 (first time used in an operating room, not for the patient's sake but to protect a nurse with skin allergies)

X-rays: 1895

Blood transfusion: 1905

Antibiotics: 1939

PRESIDENTIAL ASSASSINS
Lincoln: John Wilkes Booth
Garfield: Charles J. Guiteau
McKinley: Leon Czolgosz
Kennedy: Lee Harvey Oswald (?)

1917
Protection of president's immediate family

1962
Protection of vice presidents

1965
Protection of former presidents and spouses for life

1997
Presidents elected after January 1997 have protection for only ten years after leaving office

CHARLES DARWIN

WHAT, ME WORRY?

Naturalist and Author
Born: Shropshire, England,
February 12, 1809
Died: Downe, England,
April 19, 1882
73 years old

CHARLES DARWIN IS famous for his theory of evolution. He figured out that living things evolve over millions of years and that only the strongest survive. Unfortunately, he was one of the weaker ones. He was a sweet man, but he was anxious, constantly nauseated, and afraid to leave his house. He had it bad. If anyone came to see him, he would run behind a curtain and throw up.

Darwin's biggest worry was about his theory of evolution. It went against every religious belief of the time, and he knew it wouldn't go over as easy as, say, the theory of gravity. So he didn't tell a soul about it for twenty years. And keeping the biggest biological secret of all time made him as sick as a dog, until his heart couldn't take it anymore.

As a boy, Darwin bagged beetles, collected crud off boat bottoms, and scraped moss from trees for fun. He kept lists of everything he 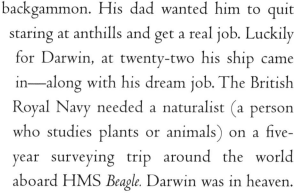 shot, touched, and played, like his 2,795 wins at backgammon. His dad wanted him to quit staring at anthills and get a real job. Luckily for Darwin, at twenty-two his ship came in—along with his dream job. The British Royal Navy needed a naturalist (a person who studies plants or animals) on a five-year surveying trip around the world aboard HMS *Beagle*. Darwin was in heaven. Wherever they landed, he collected stuff. He sent home 5,436 specimens to study.

But that expedition was the last outdoor adventure for Darwin. He went home and never left. Within a year of returning, Darwin had figured out that every species evolved from a single form of life. While he tried to prove it, he spent a lot of time upchucking, fretting, panting for air, farting, shivering, and avoiding people. Along the way, Darwin published pleasing nature books and, on the sly, wrote the most revolutionary ideas about life on earth anyone ever thought. He was a genius, but a few cards short of a full deck. He had all the aces, but he was low on 7s, 8s, and 9s.

Darwin married his first cousin Emma Wedgwood. People married first cousins back then without knowing better, but Darwin worried about the possible consequences. They spawned ten offspring: two died as babies, one died at ten, one never talked, and one didn't move. Darwin's house was like a little hospital where Emma played head nurse. His survival-of-the-fittest theory played out perfectly within his own family; only three of his kids were able to reproduce.

On the Origin of Species was published in 1859 and it sold out immediately, but the Victorian religious community was furious about his ideas, just as he had expected.

For fifty years Darwin suffered from nausea, headaches, dizziness, numbness, boils, eczema, palpitations, insomnia, depression, and gas (this is the short list)—all of which he logged in a daily health diary. The guy barfed after every meal and a few times every night.

He tried everything to keep a meal down, including poisonous concoctions made with strychnine, which didn't help. Neither did Bitter Indian ale, Condy's Ozonised Fluid, bismuth, opium, chalk, or carbonate of ammonia. His doctors looped battery-charged brass and zinc wires around his upper body and then splashed him with vinegar, but that didn't work, either—not to mention the ugly marks it left all over his chest.

After all else failed, Darwin forced himself to put away his microscope and leave his house to go to the famous Dr. Gully's Water-Cure Spa. There, he was wrapped like a mummy in sopping wet sheets and laid out on a wooden board until the sheets dried hours later. Then they rubbed and slapped his body with towels until his skin glowed red. He had heat-lamp baths to make him sweat like a pig and icy baths that froze his tail off. They aimed 650 gallons of freezing cold water at his spine and shot it through a narrow pipe. His legs erupted in boils. That was considered a sign of success. He called it his "delightful water cure."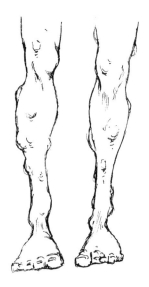

Darwin didn't throw up for thirty whole days! But maybe he just felt better because his regular activities of leaning over a vat of formaldehyde, skinning dead ducks with his bare hands, or having stare-downs with stuffed squirrels came to a dead halt. For fifty years Darwin inhaled the fumes of science and poked his fingers in everything. He didn't wear a mask or special gloves, and his work area wasn't ventilated properly. But his doctors never imagined that those things could have made him sick.

The doctors couldn't find anything officially wrong with any part of him—until he started having seizures. Aha! Finally they knew something, but it was bad news. Blood to his heart was blocked. He had angina. There was nothing they could do.

Darwin was an old man by then. Emma made sure he stopped working. He logged his four millionth puke and noted his intestinal gas after dinner (as did his family). Darwin was going the way of all flesh, and of all bug, reptile, and rhododendron. His clock was winding down, and the end was near. Darwin was evolving into a dead man. "I'm not the least afraid to die," he said.

Darwin was sick, but he wanted to keep working. One day he received in the mail, from a fellow biologist, a water beetle with a

138

bivalve (clam) stuck to it, and he was excited. Emma finally agreed to let him go catalog his new specimen. That day he felt good.

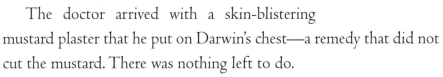

A few days later, Darwin got into bed. Pain seized his chest. He was given brandy to kill the pain but, as with everything else, he had trouble keeping it down.

The doctor arrived with a skin-blistering mustard plaster that he put on Darwin's chest—a remedy that did not cut the mustard. There was nothing left to do.

Poor Darwin. His chest pain was excruciating. He heaved and shuddered. His skin grew cold and took on a ghostly gray shade. Bright red blood came out of his mouth and ran down his white beard. Emma stayed with him.

Had he been able, he may have wanted to write in his health diary: *Emma rocked me in her arms. It was nice. I was tired. I died.*

Charles Darwin had a heart attack and died on April 19, 1882. He was seventy-three years old.

Darwin wanted to be buried in the local graveyard next to his dead children. All controversy aside, his theory of evolution had made him a national treasure. Government officials asked the family if they wished to bury Darwin in Westminster Abbey in London, near Isaac Newton, the man who came up with the theory of gravity. It was an offer they couldn't refuse.

PHOBIAS

A PHOBIA IS A STRONG, irrational fear of something that can sometimes cause breathlessness, nausea, dizziness, and anxiety.

Apiphobia: fear of bees
Arachibutyrophobia: fear of peanut butter sticking to the roof of the mouth
Arithmophobia: fear of numbers
Barophobia: fear of gravity
Deipnophobia: fear of dining with others
Emetophobia: fear of vomiting
Gelotophobia: fear of being laughed at
Hippopotomonstrosesquippedaliophobia: fear of long words
Nephophobia: fear of clouds
Olfactophobia: fear of smells
Panophobia: fear of everything
Papaphobia: fear of the pope
Pupaphobia: fear of puppets
Testophobia: fear of taking tests
Tonitrophobia: fear of thunder

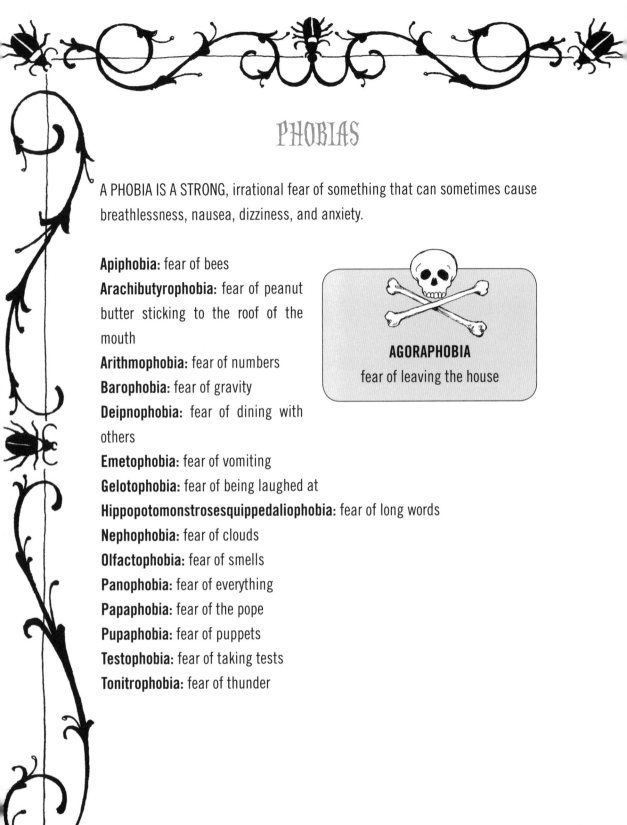

AGORAPHOBIA
fear of leaving the house

MAP OF THE HMS BEAGLE TRIP

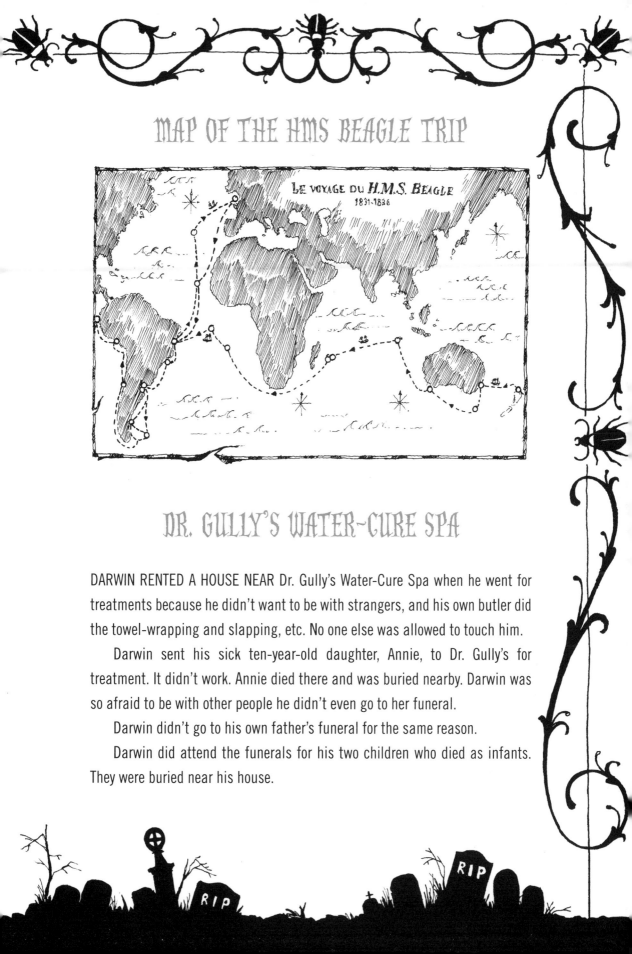

LE VOYAGE DU *H.M.S. BEAGLE*
1831-1836

DR. GULLY'S WATER-CURE SPA

DARWIN RENTED A HOUSE NEAR Dr. Gully's Water-Cure Spa when he went for treatments because he didn't want to be with strangers, and his own butler did the towel-wrapping and slapping, etc. No one else was allowed to touch him.

Darwin sent his sick ten-year-old daughter, Annie, to Dr. Gully's for treatment. It didn't work. Annie died there and was buried nearby. Darwin was so afraid to be with other people he didn't even go to her funeral.

Darwin didn't go to his own father's funeral for the same reason.

Darwin did attend the funerals for his two children who died as infants. They were buried near his house.

MARIE CURIE

YOU GLOW, GIRL

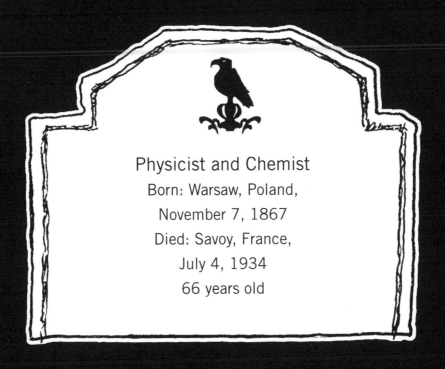

Physicist and Chemist
Born: Warsaw, Poland,
November 7, 1867
Died: Savoy, France,
July 4, 1934
66 years old

TO SAY THAT science was Marie Curie's life is an understatement. Science was more important to her than people, money, sleeping, and eating. She definitely wasn't the woman you called to have a bunch of laughs with. She couldn't. She had to be a superwoman to make it in the male-dominated field of science.

One day, Marie saw something glowing on this stuff called uranium. She wanted to know, what's that? To figure out what was glowing, Marie had eight tons of mountainous rubble known as pitchblende hauled in carts and dumped at the door of her school lab. It took Marie four years to boil, coax, and reduce this glowing pile down to one-fifth of a teaspoon of pure magic. Imagine that. She had turned a mountain into a molehill of radium. She called it "my child." Marie Curie gave life to a new element, but that element drained the life out of her.

Marie was born in Poland. Her life theory was: work slowly, never forget anything, and never make a mistake. The word "leisure" was not in her vocabulary. She went to the Sorbonne in France because there was no such thing as college for girls in Poland. Although she was pretty, she didn't care that her clothes were shabby or that she lived in a dump—all that mattered were her grades.

Marie met the French scientist Pierre Curie. They talked about crystallography and piezoelectric quartz and other romantic things that only the two of them could comprehend, and they got married. Her wedding dress wasn't white; it was dark and practical so that afterward she could wear it straight to the lab. They had two children, but Marie spent more time with her radium child than with her own girls.

Marie worked with radium day in and day out for almost nine years. Radium was beautiful. It glowed with supernatural energy, as if fairies had touched it. It was radioactive. It could help cure cancer.

Marie and Pierre won the Nobel Prize in physics together with Antoine Henri Becquerel. But the Curies were too sick to pick up their prize. Marie had lost fifteen pounds, her fingertips were black, and her face looked like it was dusted with flour. And Pierre could barely walk.

144

One day, Pierre couldn't get out of the way of a horse-drawn cab, and he was killed.

Marie's life and lab partner was gone, and she was heartbroken. But she was also a maniac workaholic, so she went right back to work. She became the first woman professor at the Sorbonne, and she taught Radioactivity 101.

Superwoman Marie won her second Nobel Prize, this time for chemistry. And then she spent a few years driving X-ray machines around in a truck during World War I, helping doctors locate bullets inside wounded soldiers. Back at the lab, with a beaker and a Bunsen burner, she tried to find uses for radioactive materials in medicine.

But Marie was in need of some medicine herself. Her blackened fingertips were cracked and oozing, and she incessantly rubbed them together. There was a loud buzz in her ears, and she looked like a bag of bones in a ghost mask. Double cataracts made her practically blind. Like I was saying, no laughs here.

It wasn't just Marie who was getting sick. One of her radioactivity students had his whole arm amputated. Fifteen young women who had painted radium on clock dials died.

145

Marie was losing her power. She was running dangerously short of the red blood cells that carried oxygen to her muscles and brain. Her entire body hurt, and her smart thinking was becoming not so smart.

Marie ignored the obvious: radium was kryptonite to superwoman Curie; it depleted her power. But she kept holding test tubes with her bare hands and using a straw in her mouth to move toxic ingredients from vessel to vessel.

One day at the lab, Marie spiked a fever that even she couldn't ignore. Her whole body stalled out; her bone marrow had shut down. She was running on her last tank of blood, and there'd be no more fill-ups.

Marie Curie died in France on July 4, 1934. The cause of death was aplastic anemia caused by continuous exposure to radiation. She was sixty-six years old.

Marie never let on whether she knew that her beautiful glowing child had killed her. Except maybe on her deathbed. She kept saying that all she needed to recover was a dose of fresh air. She was right . . . it was just way too late.

To this day, Marie Curie continues to be a glowing beacon for girls pursuing a life in science—along with her work desk, which will glow for fifteen hundred years to come.

APLASTIC ANEMIA

THIS IS A CONDITION IN which bone marrow does not make enough new cells to replenish the blood. It causes lower counts in red blood cells, white blood cells, and platelets. Symptoms include lack of energy, unhealthy paleness, palpitations, and easy bruising.

The most common cause is exposure to toxins and unprotected exposure to radioactive material.

RADIOLUMINESCENT PAINT

RADIOLUMINESCENT PAINT GLOWED IN THE dark. It was made of radioactive material mixed with luminescent crystalline powder.

It was first used in 1902 to paint clock dials. By 1920 more than four million watches and clocks had been painted. Also painted were house numbers, bedroom slippers, fish bait, theater seat numbers, pistol sights, and eyes on dolls.

Radioactive materials in paint have been discontinued since the 1970s.

MARIE CURIE
IN MEMORIAM

"Her strength, her purity of will, her austerity toward herself, her objectivity, her incorruptible judgment—all these were of a kind seldom found joined in a single individual. . . . Once she had recognized a certain way as the right one, she pursued it without compromise and with extreme tenacity."

—ALBERT EINSTEIN, Curie Memorial Celebration
at the Roerich Museum, New York, November 23, 1935

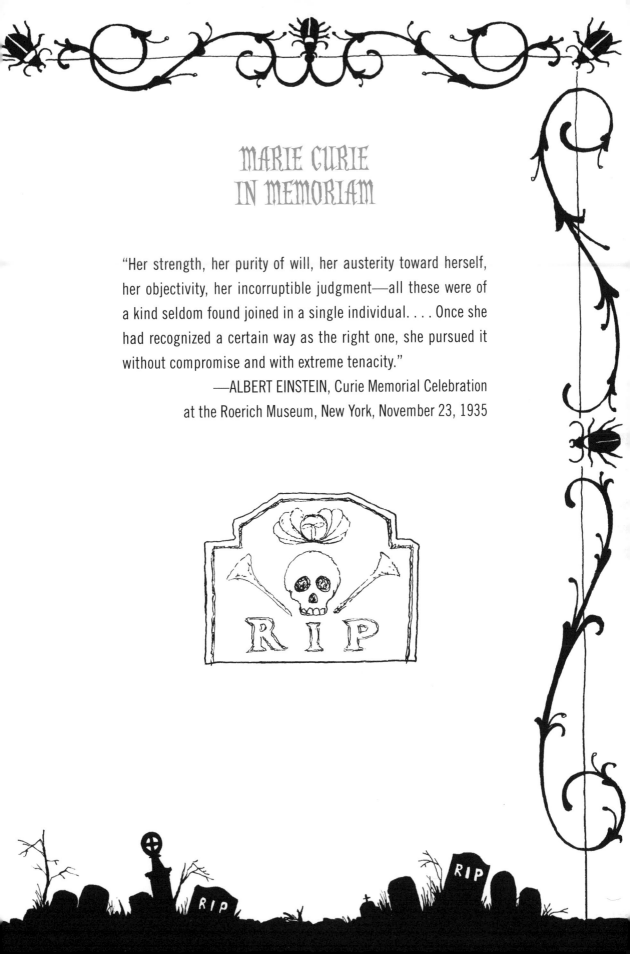

ALBERT EINSTEIN

EINSTEIN ≈ MASSIVE CRANIUM?

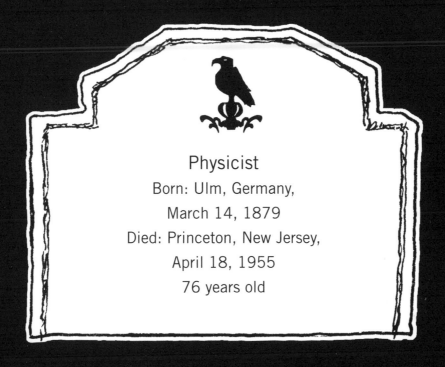

Physicist
Born: Ulm, Germany,
March 14, 1879
Died: Princeton, New Jersey,
April 18, 1955
76 years old

ALBERT EINSTEIN MADE physics look fun and kind of silly. He smiled a lot, forgot to comb his hair, and rode his bike while he was unlocking the secrets of the universe. He made equations like $E = mc^2$ seem easy and beautiful, but it's hard work to think up something that simple. A normal brain has twenty-five million neurons linked by billions of connections, and ideas run through miles of nerve fibers at two hundred miles per hour. Maybe Einstein had more neurons or maybe his ideas moved faster. Or maybe his brain was just bigger than everybody else's. Einstein himself shrugged off his smarts. "A new idea comes suddenly and in a rather intuitive way," he said.

Einstein was born in Germany, into a Jewish family. His mom noticed that his head was fat, with weird angles. He didn't even speak until he was three, but his chubby noggin was the right size for soaking up geometry and science. Pretty soon Einstein's big head was outthinking his teachers. He dropped out of high school and went to a polytechnic institute in Switzerland to see what he could learn someplace else. But once a student there, he spent a lot of time *not* going to class. Einstein's lab was his own brain.

Einstein was only twenty-six when he came up with the general theory of relativity. His paper on photoelectric effect earned him the Nobel Prize. Everybody wanted a piece of him. His ideas were in demand, and he was given honorary doctorate degrees in science, medicine, and philosophy from universities all over the world.

But the world was at war a lot of the time. During World War I, Einstein became a pacifist. He believed in a world government. A few years before World War II, Einstein left Germany and moved to the United States.

He spent twenty-two years at Princeton University teaching and doing research. He grew old, and he had great pain in his stomach. Even with the best medical care, the inevitable happened. The abdominal aorta, the main artery of the heart, which leads to the stomach, stretched out like a balloon and started to leak.

Albert Einstein died in New Jersey on April 18, 1955, of an aortic aneurysm: a burst artery. He was seventy-six years old. The world's most famous genius and humanitarian was dead. He had expressed a wish to be cremated.

But before that happened, Einstein's body was examined in a so-called routine autopsy. The pathologist on duty, Thomas Harvey, couldn't believe his luck when he saw Einstein's chilled corpse splayed out on the steel table.

First, he sliced Einstein's body open right down the middle. The rib cage that had protected Einstein's insides for almost eight decades was jimmied open. With tweezers, clippers, pruning shears, a bone saw, and various other tools of the trade, the pathologist examined Einstein's guts. His liver, lungs, kidneys, heart, and all sorts of glands and filter systems were detached and lined up on a table.

The pathologist confirmed the cause of Einstein's death. The completely unnecessary postmortem was complete. But Harvey's stars had aligned in a way that he refused to ignore. This was his moment to be famous.

"It's not every day you get a genius to autopsy," he said later. Einstein's face still looked just like Einstein (in a waxy sort of way). One plus about corpses is that they feel no pain. So when Harvey parted Einstein's hair neatly across the top of his head, sliced open the scalp from ear to ear, and folded it over Einstein's face and down his neck, it was painless for all concerned.

He cut Einstein's skull in half, just above the eyebrows, with a special electric saw that shut down when it sensed soft tissue. Then, with the skull chisel wedged in place and a few whacks of a mallet, Einstein's cranium came off with a sticky, sucking sound.

153

His spinal cord and everything else that wired Einstein's think tank to the rest of him was snipped free. Against the deceased's wishes, and without permission from the next of kin, Harvey reached in and removed Einstein's brain. The pathologist couldn't wait to measure it. He would forever be the man who had confirmed what everybody already figured—Einstein's brain was larger than everybody else's. It had to be.

Harvey placed Einstein's noodle in the grocery scale hanging from the ceiling. The brain weighed 2.7 pounds, the weight of a head of cabbage. That's a tad *less* than the average brain. What? That couldn't be right! The pathologist didn't want to give up his chance at fame too fast, so he plopped Einstein's brain into a jar of formaldehyde.

The guy stuffed cotton in the now-empty black hole in Einstein's skull. The top of the cranium was set back in place, and it stayed put after Einstein's peeled face and scalp were sewn back together. The pathologist arranged Einstein's hair in a really bad old-man comb-over to hide the stitches. The organs were returned to the torso, and Einstein's chest was stitched together like a seam on a baseball.

154

Thomas Harvey met with the press and reported his findings. He didn't mention that Einstein's brain was now floating in a jar in the body-parts room. And when Harvey got back to the autopsy room, Einstein's mangled remains were off to be cremated.

At the crematorium, the mourners didn't notice their loved one's upper story had been gutted of all its marbles. Einstein's oh-so-light body was cremated, and the ashes were scattered somewhere in New Jersey.

Harvey told his boss and boasted to his family that he had Einstein's brain. That kind of news travels fast. Einstein's son, Hans Albert, found out someone had stolen his dad's brain when he read about it in the newspaper. He was furious and called the hospital, but somehow the pathologist talked Hans Albert into letting him keep the Brain of the Century. He promised Hans Albert he would use it in a scientific study.

The hospital didn't see it that way and fired Harvey. So Harvey took the brain home. After all, Hans Albert had given it to him. In his spare time, Harvey photographed Einstein's intact noodle before he cut it in half and sliced it, luncheon-meat thin, into 240 pieces, then embedded the slices on microscope slides. The leftover brain chunks filled three jars. Years and years went by. Einstein's brain spent a few decades in Harvey's basement, in a beer cooler. It also took a trip across the country in the trunk of Harvey's car.

Harvey didn't know the first thing about how to study the brain, nor was he able to get anyone else to do it. He sent slides through the mail to various brain researchers without his return address, and he never followed up.

Thirty years later, in 1985, one of the researchers who had received blobs of Einstein's gray matter discovered that his brain had more cells than normal brains. But no one is sure if that's what made him so smart.

After keeping Einstein's brain for forty years, Harvey finally found someone to study it: Sandra Witelson at McMaster University in Hamilton, Ontario, Canada. He gave her fourteen pieces of brain and his original photographs. She concluded that Einstein's inferior parietal region, the area associated with visual and spatial reasoning, was 15 percent larger than normal and he didn't have a Sylvian fissure (a particular crevice) like you and I have. So instead of two key brain sections, Einstein had one big section.

That study was done using Harvey's photographs and autopsy measurements, not the brain itself. Harvey could have returned the brain to its rightful owner after photographing and measuring it. Stealing something is always a stupid choice. Before Harvey

156

died in 2007, he drove Einstein's brain back to Princeton Hospital and gave it to the pathologist who held his old job. The brain is still there.

Einstein's theories continue to astound physicists today. But before he died, he offered up another theory: "Our death is not an end if we can live on in our children and the younger generation. For they are us, our bodies are only wilted leaves on the tree of life."

EINSTEIN'S EYEBALLS

HENRY ABRAMS, AN EYE SURGEON, spent a few minutes with Einstein's corpse. With his bare hands he opened Einstein's eyelids, snipped Einstein's eyeballs free, and took them out with a pair of forceps. He dropped them into a jar of formaldehyde and took them home.

Abrams still has them. Einstein's eyeballs are in a bank safe-deposit box somewhere in New Jersey.

CREMATION 101

TO CREMATE IS TO BURN a corpse by fire. Here's how:

1. Remove jewelry, gold fillings, pacemakers, prosthetics, and any mechanical implants. They won't burn, and they might ruin the cremation chamber.
2. Set a fire between 1,400 and 1,800 degrees Fahrenheit.
3. Make sure the body is burning properly. If not, move it around.
4. Wait one and a half to three hours, depending on the body's size.
5. Let the ashes cool.
6. Sweep the ashes out of the chamber. (There will be some commingling with the ashes of previously cremated bodies.)
7. Get an urn large enough to hold between three and nine pounds of whitish ash.

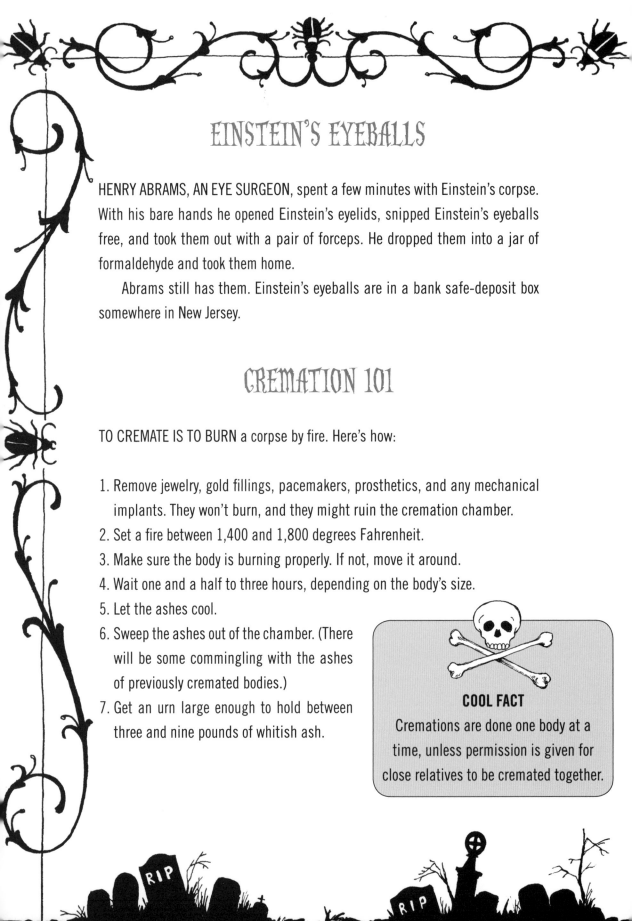

COOL FACT
Cremations are done one body at a time, unless permission is given for close relatives to be cremated together.

NOTABLE EINSTEIN QUOTES

"Why is it that nobody understands me, and everybody likes me?"

"With fame I become more and more stupid, which of course is a very common phenomenon."

"I have no special talents. I am only passionately curious."

"Look deep, deep into nature, and then you will understand everything better."

"There is only one road to true human greatness: through the school of hard knocks."

"If you want to live a happy life, tie it to a goal, not to people or things."

"We must . . . dedicate our lives to drying up the source of war: ammunition factories."

ONE MORE THING

THE PEOPLE IN this book didn't become famous because of how they croaked but because of how they lived. A passion, a belief in themselves, and hard work made them historic and unforgettable. Just think: Caesar, Columbus, Elizabeth I, Galileo, Mozart, Beethoven, Poe, Dickens, Darwin, Curie, and Einstein all worked until the day they died. They loved what they were doing so much, it probably didn't feel like work at all—they were just playing.

These icons from all over the world—and centuries apart—influenced one another, and coincidences linked them in unexpected ways. Mozart listened to Beethoven play the piano. Marie Antoinette watched Mozart play. Marie Antoinette's beheading paved the way for Napoleon's rule over France. Napoleon and his men found the Rosetta stone, which deciphered hieroglyphics, including the writing of King Tut's era. Caesar and Cleopatra hung out together. Dickens read Poe and Poe read Dickens. And Einstein listened to Mozart's music for inspiration.

Some we admire more than others, but there is one thing to learn from each of their stories: whether your dream is to study worms or to live in a space station, to be a lawyer, the number-one tennis player, or to paint pictures, it's up to you. Whatever your story is, if what you are doing is so much fun it feels like you're just playing, you are onto something very important. When you feel that way, you are doing what you're meant to do. Don't let anyone talk you out of it.

Because, guess what?

Eventually, everybody's story ends.

And now, so does this book.

CONNECTIONS

THE LIVES OF these important historical figures intersected in some fascinating ways.

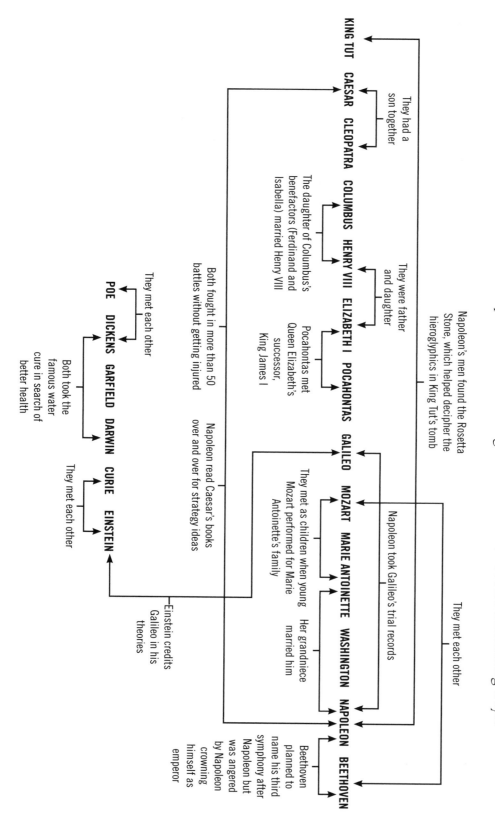

KING TUT

CAESAR

CLEOPATRA

COLUMBUS

HENRY VIII

ELIZABETH I

POCAHONTAS

GALILEO

MOZART

MARIE ANTOINETTE

WASHINGTON

NAPOLEON

BEETHOVEN

POE

DICKENS

GARFIELD

DARWIN

CURIE

EINSTEIN

They had a son together

They were father and daughter

The daughter of Columbus's benefactors (Ferdinand and Isabella) married Henry VIII

Pocahontas met Queen Elizabeth's successor, King James I

They met each other

Both fought in more than 50 battles without getting injured

Napoleon read Caesar's books over and over for strategy ideas

Napoleon's men found the Rosetta Stone, which helped decipher the hieroglyphics in King Tut's tomb

Napoleon took Galileo's trial records

They met each other

They met as children when young Mozart performed for Marie Antoinette's family

Her grandniece married him

Einstein credits Galileo in his theories

Both took the famous water cure in search of better health

They met each other

Beethoven planned to name his third symphony after Napoleon but was angered by Napoleon crowning himself as emperor

ACKNOWLEDGMENTS

THANKS TO Edward Necarsulmer IV for knowing that a book of gory facts would be worth writing, and for his wisdom in finding Emily Easton, the perfect editor for it.

This book would have died a quick death without the wise advice of Jennie Bragg, Leah Komaiko, Victoria Beck, Christine Bernardi, Tracy Holczer, Leslie Margolis, Elizabeth Passarelli, Anne Reinhard, Angela Wiencek, and Cathleen Young.

SOURCES

KING TUT

Boyer, Richard S., R. C. Connolly, Todd C. Grey, and Ernst A. Rodin. "The Skull and Cervical Spine Radiographs of Tutankhamen: A Critical Appraisal." *American Journal of Neuroradiology.* Salt Lake City, UT: The Neuroradiology Education and Research Foundation, 2003.

Budge, E. A. Wallis. *The Mummy.* New York: Collier Books, 1972.

Carter, Howard. *The Tomb of Tutankhamen.* New York: Cooper Square Publishers, 1963.

Cartwright, Frederick F. *The Development of Modern Surgery.* New York: Thomas Y. Crowell Company, 1968.

Cooper, Gregory M., and Michael R. King. *Who Killed King Tut? Using Modern Forensics to Solve a 3,300-Year-Old Mystery.* New York: Prometheus Books, 2004.

Doherty, P. C. *The Mysterious Death of Tutankhamun.* New York: Carroll & Graf, 2002.

El Mahdy, Christine. *Tutankhamen: The Life and Death of the Boy-King.* New York: St. Martin's Press, 1999.

Grosser, Maurice. *The Painter's Eye.* New York: The New American Library of World Literature, Inc., 1951.

Hawass, Zahi. *Tutankhamun and the Golden Age of the Pharaohs.* Washington DC: National Geographic Society, 2005.

Hawass, Zahi. "Tutankhamun CT Scan." Press Release. 2005. www.drhawass.com

Leca, Ange-Pierre. *The Egyptian Way of Death: Mummies and the Cult of the Immortal.* New York: Doubleday, 1981.

Parkinson, Richard. *Pocket Guide to Ancient Egyptian Hieroglyphs.* New York: Barnes & Noble Books, 2003.

Stanek, Steven. "King Tut's Mummy to Be Displayed for 1st Time." *National Geographic News,* 2007.

Stierlin, Henri. *The Gold of the Pharaohs.* Paris: Editions Pierre Terrail, 2003.

Wilford, John Noble. "Malaria Is a Likely Killer in King Tut's Post-Mortem." *The New York Times,* February 16, 2010.

JULIUS CAESAR

Balsdon, J. P. V. D. *Julius Caesar: A Political Biography.* New York: Atheneum, 1967.

Canfora, Luciano. *Julius Caesar: The Life and Times of the People's Dictator.* Berkeley: University of California Press, 2007.

Goodman, Martin. *The Roman World: 44 BC–AD 180.* New York: Routledge, 1997.

Johnson, Paul. *Heroes: From Alexander the Great and Julius Caesar to Churchill and de Gaulle.* New York: HarperCollins Publishers, 2007.

Parenti, Michael. *The Assassination of Julius Caesar: A People's History of Ancient Rome.* New York: The New Press, 2003.

CLEOPATRA

Bell, Gail. *Poison: A History and a Family Memoir.* New York: St. Martin's Press, 2001.

Chauveau, Michel. *Cleopatra: Beyond the Myth.* Ithaca, NY: Cornell University Press, 2002.

Empereur, Jean-Yves. *Alexandria Rediscovered.* New York: G. Braziller, 1998.

Emsley, John. *Elements of Murder.* New York: Oxford University Press, 2005.

Foreman, Laura. *Cleopatra's Palace: In Search of a Legend.* New York: Discovery Books, 1999.

Grant, Michael. *Cleopatra.* London: Phoenix Press, 2000.

Kleiner, Diana E. E. *Cleopatra and Rome.* Cambridge, MA: Belknap Press of Harvard University Press, 2005.

CHRISTOPHER COLUMBUS

Brinkbäumer, Klaus, and Clemens Höges. *The Voyage of the Vizcaina: The Mystery of Christopher Columbus's Last Ship.* Orlando, FL: Harcourt, 2006.

Carpenter, Kenneth J. *The History of Scurvy and Vitamin C.* New York: Cambridge University Press, 1986.

Columbus, Christopher. *The Log of Christopher Columbus' First Voyage to America in the Year 1492.* Hamden, CT: Linnet Books, 1989.

Dugard, Martin. *The Last Voyage of Columbus: Being the Epic Tale of the Great Captain's Fourth Expedition, Including Accounts of Swordfight, Mutiny, Shipwreck, Gold, War, Hurricane, and Discovery.* New York: Little, Brown and Company, 2005.

Granzotto, Gianni. *Christopher Columbus.* New York: Doubleday, 1985.

Morison, Samuel Eliot. *Admiral of the Ocean Sea: A Life of Christopher Columbus.* Boston: Little, Brown and Company, 1942.

Weissmann, Gerald. *They All Laughed at Christopher Columbus: Tales of Medicine and the Art of Discovery.* New York: Times Books, 1987.

Wilford, John Noble. *The Mysterious History of Columbus: An Exploration of the Man, the Myth, the Legacy.* New York: Alfred A. Knopf, 1991.

HENRY VIII

Bowle, John. *Henry VIII: A Biography.* Boston: Little, Brown and Company, 1964.

Brinch, Ove. "The Medical Problems of Henry VIII." In *Tenements of Clay: An Anthology of Medical Biographical Essays.* New York: Charles Scribner's Sons, 1974.

Bruce, Marie Louise. *The Making of Henry VIII*. New York: Coward, McCann & Geoghegan, 1977.

Cohen, Bertram. "King Henry VIII and the Barber Surgeons." *Annals of the Royal College of Surgeons of England*. Vol. 40; London: Dorriston House, 1967.

Erickson, Carolly. *Great Harry*. New York: Summit Books, 1980.

Morrison, Brysson. *The Private Life of Henry VIII*. New York: Vanguard Press, Inc., 1964.

Starkey, David. *Six Wives: The Queens of Henry VIII*. New York: HarperCollins Publishers, 2003.

Weir, Alison. *The Children of Henry VIII*. New York: Ballantine Books, 1996.

Weir, Alison. *Henry VIII: The King and His Court*. New York: Ballantine Books, 2001.

Weir, Alison. *The Six Wives of Henry VIII*. New York: Grove Press, 1991.

Williams, Neville. *Henry VIII and His Court*. New York: The Macmillan Company, 1971.

ELIZABETH I

Dunn, Jane. *Elizabeth and Mary: Cousins, Rivals, Queens*. New York: Alfred A. Knopf, 2003.

Jenkins, Elizabeth. *Elizabeth the Great*. New York: Coward-McCann, Inc., 1959.

Johnson, Paul. *Heroes: From Alexander the Great and Julius Caesar to Churchill and de Gaulle*. New York: HarperCollins Publishers, 2007.

Loades, D. M. *Elizabeth I*. London: Hambledon and London, 2003.

Plowden, Alison. *The Young Elizabeth: The First Twenty-five Years of Elizabeth I*. Stroud, Gloucestershire: Sutton Publishing Ltd., 1999.

Ridley, Jasper. *Elizabeth I: The Shrewdness of Virtue*. New York: Viking Penguin Inc., 1987.

Strachey, Lytton. *Elizabeth and Essex*. New York: Harcourt, Brace and Company, 1928.

Weir, Alison. *The Children of Henry VIII*. New York: Ballantine Books, 2008.

Weir, Alison. *The Life of Elizabeth I*. New York: Ballantine Books, 1998.

POCAHONTAS

Ackerknecht, Erwin H. *History and Geography of the Most Important Diseases*. New York: Hafner Publishing Company, Inc., 1965.

Allen, Paula Gunn. *Pocahontas: Medicine Woman, Spy, Entrepreneur, Diplomat*. San Francisco: HarperCollins Publishers, 2003.

Custalow, Dr. Linwood. "Little Bear." In *The True Story of Pocahontas: The Other Side of History*. Colorado: Fulcrum Publishing, 2007.

Daniel, Angela L. "Silver Star." In *The True Story of Pocahontas: The Other Side of History*. Colorado: Fulcrum Publishing, 2007.

Hume, Ivor Noel. *The Virginia Adventure: Roanoke to James Towne: An Archaeological and Historical Odyssey*. New York: Alfred A. Knopf, 1994.

Kelso, William M. *Jamestown, the Buried Truth.* Charlottesville, VA: University of Virginia Press, 2006.

Mossiker, Frances. *Pocahontas: The Life and the Legend.* New York: Alfred A. Knopf, 1967.

Price, David A. *Love and Hate in Jamestown.* New York: Alfred A. Knopf, 2003.

Townsend, Camilla. *Pocahontas and the Powhatan Dilemma.* New York: Hill and Wang, 2004.

GALILEO GALILEI

Bragg, Melvyn. *On Giants' Shoulders: Great Scientists and Their Discoveries—from Archimedes to DNA.* London: Hodder & Stoughton, 1998.

Drake, Stillman. *Galileo: Pioneer Scientist.* Toronto: University of Toronto Press, 1994.

Finocchiaro, Maurice A. *Retrying Galileo.* Berkeley: University of California Press, 2005.

Machamer, Peter. *The Cambridge Companion to Galileo.* New York: Cambridge University Press, 1998.

Porter, Roy, and G. S. Rousseau. *Gout: The Patrician Malady.* New Haven and London: Yale University Press, 1998.

Redondi, Pietro. *Galileo: Heretic.* Princeton, NJ: Princeton University Press, 1967.

Rowland, Wade. *Galileo's Mistake.* New York: Arcade Publishing, 2003.

Sobel, Dava. *Galileo's Daughter: A Historical Memoir of Science, Faith, and Love.* New York: Walker & Company, 1999.

Weissmann, Gerald. *Galileo's Gout: Science in an Age of Endarkenment.* New York: Bellevue Literary Press, 2007.

WOLFGANG AMADEUS MOZART

Bakalar, Nicholas. "What Really Killed Mozart? Maybe Strep." *The New York Times,* August 18, 2009.

Davenport, Marcia. *Mozart.* New York: Barnes & Noble Books, 1995.

Gay, Peter. *Mozart.* New York: Viking, 1999.

Glover, Jane. *Mozart's Women: His Family, His Friends, His Music.* New York: HarperCollins Publishers, 2005.

Guillery, Edward N. "Did Mozart Die of Kidney Disease? A Review from the Bicentennial of His Death." *Journal of the American Society of Nephrology.* 1992; 2:1671–1676.

Hildesheimer, Wolfgang. *Mozart.* New York: Farrar, Straus and Giroux, 1982.

Landon, H. C. Robbins. *Mozart's Last Year.* New York: Schirmer Books, 1988.

Mozart, Wolfgang Amadeus. *Mozart's Letters, Mozart's Life.* Robert Spaethling, ed. New York: W. W. Norton, 2000.

Ross, Alex. "The Storm of Style: Listening to the Complete Mozart." *The New Yorker,* July 24, 2006.

Rushton, Julian. *Mozart.* New York: Oxford University Press, 2006.

Solomon, Maynard. *Mozart: A Life.* New York: HarperCollins Publishers, 1995.

MARIE ANTOINETTE

Campan, Jeanne Louise Henriette. *The Private Life of Marie Antoinette*. New York: Scribner and
Welford, 1887.

Fraser, Antonia. *Marie Antoinette: The Journey*. New York: Anchor Books, 2001.

Gower, Lord Ronald. *Last Days of Marie Antoinette: A Historical Sketch*. Boston: Roberts Brothers, 1892.

GEORGE WASHINGTON

Brady, Patricia. *Martha Washington: An American Life*. New York: The Viking Press, 2005.

Bumgarner, John R. "George Washington." In *The Health of the Presidents: The 41 United States
Presidents Through 1993 from a Physician's Point of View*. Jefferson, NC: McFarland & Company,
1994.

Giscard d'Estaing, Valerie-Anne. *The Second World Almanac Book of Inventions*. New York: Ballantine
Books, 1986.

Ellis, Joseph J. *His Excellency: George Washington*. New York: Alfred A. Knopf, 2004.

Evans, Dorinda. *The Genius of Gilbert Stuart*. Princeton, NJ: Princeton University Press, 1999.

Flexner, Thomas James. *George Washington: Anguish and Farewell (1793–1799)*. Boston: Little, Brown
and Company, 1972.

Henriques, Peter R. *The Death of George Washington: He Died as He Lived*. Mount Vernon, VA: The
Mount Vernon Ladies' Association, 2000.

Marx, Rudolph. *The Health of the Presidents*. New York: G. P. Putnam's Sons, 1960.

Porter, Roy. *Cambridge Illustrated History: Medicine*. Cambridge, UK: Cambridge University Press, 1996.

Randall, Sterne Willard. *George Washington: A Life*. New York: Henry Holt & Company, 1997.

Schwartz, Barry. *George Washington: The Making of an American Symbol*. New York: The Free Press, a
division of Macmillan, Inc., 1987.

Terkel, Susan Neiburg. *Colonial American Medicine*. New York: Franklin Watts, 1993.

Ward, Brian. *The Story of Medicine*. New York: Lorenz Books, 2000.

NAPOLEON BONAPARTE

Dwyer, Philip. *Napoleon: The Path to Power*. New Haven: Yale University Press, 2008.

Gengembre, Gerard. *Napoleon: The Immortal Emperor*. New York: Vendome Press, 2003.

Giles, Frank. *Napoleon Bonaparte: England's Prisoner*. New York: Carroll & Graf, 2001.

Hapgood, David, and Ben Weider. *The Murder of Napoleon*. New York: Congdon & Lattes, Inc., 1982.

Hindmarsh, Thomas J., and John Savory. "The Death of Napoleon, Cancer or Arsenic?"
Chemical Chemistry, December 1, 2008.

Johnson, Paul. *Napoleon*. New York: Penguin, 2002.

SOURCES

MacKenzie, Norman Ian. *The Escape from Elba: The Fall and Flight of Napoleon*. New York: Oxford University Press, 1982.

Walter, Jakob. *The Diary of a Napoleonic Foot Soldier*. New York: Doubleday, 1991.

LUDWIG VAN BEETHOVEN

Breuning, Gerhard von. *Memories of Beethoven: From the House of the Black-Robed Spaniards*. Cambridge, UK: Press Syndicate, 1992.

Hui, A. C. F., and S. M. Wong. "Deafness and Liver Disease in a 57-Year-Old Man: A Medical History of Beethoven." *Hong Kong Medical Journal*. Hong Kong Academy of Medicine. December 2000.

Mai, François Martin. *Diagnosing Genius: The Life and Death of Beethoven*. Montreal: McGill-Queens University Press, 2007.

Marek, George R. *Beethoven: Biography of a Genius*. New York: Funk & Wagnalls, 1996.

Martin, Russell. *Beethoven's Hair*. New York: Broadway Books, 2000.

Maugh II, Thomas H. "Research Shows Beethoven Had Lead Poisoning." *Los Angeles Times*, October 18, 2000.

Meredith, William. "The History of Beethoven's Skull Fragments." *The Beethoven Journal*. The Ira F. Brilliant Center for Beethoven Studies, San Jose State University: Summer & Winter 2005.

Ries, Ferdinand, and Franz Wegeler. *Beethoven Remembered: The Biographical Notes of Franz Wegeler and Ferdinand Ries*. Arlington, VA: Great Ocean Publishers, 1987.

Solomon, Maynard. *Late Beethoven: Music, Thought, Imagination*. Berkeley and Los Angeles: University of California Press, 2004.

Sorsby, Maurice. "Beethoven's Deafness." In *Tenements of Clay: Medical Biographies of Famous People by Modern Doctors*. New York: Charles Scribner's Sons, 1974.

EDGAR ALLAN POE

Ackroyd, Peter. *Poe: A Life Cut Short*. New York: Nan A. Talese, 2008.

Bloom, Harold. *Edgar Allan Poe: Comprehensive Research and Study Guide*. Broomall, PA: Chelsea House Publishers, 1999.

Bloom, Harold. *The Tales of Poe*. New York: Chelsea House Publishers, 1987.

Hayes, Kevin J. *The Cambridge Companion to Edgar Allan Poe*. New York: Cambridge University Press, 2002.

Hutchisson, James M. *Poe*. Jackson, MS: University Press of Mississippi, 2005.

Lepore, Jill. "The Humbug: Edgar Allan Poe and the Economy of Horror." *The New Yorker*, April 27, 2009.

Meltzer, Milton. *Edgar Allan Poe: A Biography*. Minneapolis, MN: Twenty-First Century Books, 2003.

"Poe's Death Is Rewritten as Case of Rabies, Not Telltale Alcohol." *The New York Times*, September 15, 1996.

Savoye, Jeffrey A. "Two Biographical Digressions: Poe's Wandering Trunk and Dr. Carter's Mysterious Sword Cane." Baltimore, MD: Edgar Allan Poe Society of Baltimore, Fall 2004.

Walsh, John Evangelist. *Midnight Dreary: The Mysterious Death of Edgar Allan Poe.* Piscataway, NJ: Rutgers University Press, 1998.

CHARLES DICKENS

Bowen, W. H. *Charles Dickens and His Family.* Cambridge, UK: W. Heffer & Sons Ltd., 1956.

Epstein, Norrie. *The Friendly Dickens.* New York: Penguin Books, 1998.

Fido, Martin. *Charles Dickens: An Authentic Account of His Life & Times.* New York: Hamlyn Publishers, 1973.

Forster, John. *The Life of Charles Dickens.* London: Chapman & Hall, 1874.

Dickens, Sir Henry Fielding. *Memories of My Father.* Great Britain: Duffield & Company, 1929.

Dickens, Mamie. *My Father as I Recall Him.* New York: Dutton, 1897.

Kaplan, Fred. *Dickens: A Biography.* New York: William Morrow and Co., 1988.

Magill, Frank N. *Masterplots: Cyclopedia of Literary Characters.* New York: Salem Press, Inc., 1963.

Mankowitz, Wolf. *Dickens of London.* New York: Macmillan Publishing Co., Inc., 1977.

Paroissien, David. *Selected Letters of Charles Dickens.* Boston: Twayne Publishers, 1985.

Priestley, John Boyton. *Charles Dickens: A Pictorial Biography.* New York: Viking Press, 1962.

Wilson, Edmund. "The Two Scrooges." In *The Wound and the Bow: Seven Studies in Literature.* Cambridge, MA: Houghton Mifflin Company, 1941.

JAMES A. GARFIELD

Ackerman, Kenneth. *Dark Horse: The Surprise Election and Political Murder of President James A. Garfield.* New York: Carroll & Graf, 2003.

Bumgarner, John R. "James Abram Garfield." In *The Health of the Presidents: The 41 United States Presidents Through 1993 from a Physician's Point of View.* Jefferson, NC: McFarland & Company, 1994.

Marx, Rudolph. *The Health of the Presidents.* New York: G. P. Putnam's Sons, 1960.

Melanson, Philip H., with Peter F. Stevens. *The Secret Service: The Hidden History of an Enigmatic Agency.* New York: Carroll & Graf, 2002.

Rosen, Fred. *The Historical Atlas of American Crime.* New York: Checkmark Books, 2005.

Rutkow, Ira. *James A. Garfield.* New York: Henry Holt and Company, 2006.

Schaffer, Amanda. "A President Felled by an Assassin and 1880s Medical Care." *The New York Times*, July 25, 2006.

SOURCES

CHARLES DARWIN

Browne, Janet. *Charles Darwin: The Power of Place.* New York: Alfred A. Knopf, 2002.

Browne, Janet. *Charles Darwin: Voyaging.* New York: Alfred A. Knopf, 1995.

Clark, Ronald W. *The Survival of Charles Darwin: A Biography of a Man and an Idea.* New York: Random House, 1984.

Darwin, Charles. *The Autobiography of Charles Darwin: 1809–1882.* New York: Harcourt, Brace and Company, 1959.

Desmond, Adrian, and James Moore. *The Life of a Tormented Evolutionist: Darwin.* New York: Warner Books, 1991.

Hayden, Thomas. "What Darwin Didn't Know: Today's Scientists Marvel That the 19th-Century Naturalist's Grand Vision of Evolution Is Still the Key to Life." *Smithsonian,* February 2009.

Quammen, David. "Darwin's First Clues." *National Geographic,* February 2009.

Quammen, David. *The Reluctant Mr. Darwin.* New York: W. W. Norton & Company, 2006.

Shermer, Michael. *Why Darwin Matters.* New York: Henry Holt and Company, 2006.

Smith, Cameron M., and Charles Sullivan. *The Top 10 Myths about Evolution.* New York: Prometheus Books, 2007.

Stott, Rebecca. *Darwin and the Barnacle.* New York: W. W. Norton & Company, 2003.

MARIE CURIE

Curie, Eve. *Madame Curie: A Biography.* New York: Doubleday, Doran & Company, 1937.

Goldsmith, Barbara. *Obsessive Genius: The Inner World of Marie Curie.* New York: W. W. Norton & Company, 2005.

ALBERT EINSTEIN

Abraham, Carolyn. *Possessing Genius: The Bizarre Odyssey of Einstein's Brain.* Toronto: Viking, 2001.

Calaprice, Alice. *The Einstein Almanac.* Baltimore and London: The Johns Hopkins University Press, 2005.

Calaprice, Alice. *The Quotable Einstein.* Princeton, NJ: Princeton University Press, 1996.

Isaacson, Walter. *Einstein: His Life and Universe.* New York: Simon & Schuster, 2007.

Kaku, Michio. *Einstein's Cosmos.* New York: W. W. Norton & Company, 2004.

Paterniti, Michael. *Driving Mr. Albert: A Trip across America with Einstein's Brain.* New York: Dell Publishing, 2000.

FURTHER READING AND SURFING

Each section lists books, followed by websites.

KING TUT

Edwards, Roberta. *Who Was King Tut?* Illustrated by True Kelley. New York: Grosset & Dunlap, 2006.

Meltzer, Milton. *In the Days of the Pharaohs: A Look at Ancient Egypt*. New York: Franklin Watts, 2001.

http://dsc.discovery.com/egypt/tut-index.html
   The site has games, a tour of the Valley of Kings, and a link to the 3-D image of what Tut supposedly looked like according to modern science.

www2.fi.edu/tut/about.html
   Offers information about Tut's daily life, religion in Egypt at that time, Tut as the pharaoh, and Tut's death, discovery, and curse.

COOL ARTIFACT—King Tut's death mask
   http://dsc.discovery.com/egypt/tut-face/face.html

JULIUS CAESAR

Galford, Ellen. *Julius Caesar: The Boy Who Conquered an Empire*. Washington DC: National Geographic Society, 2007.

Jeffrey, Gary, and Kate Petty. *Julius Caesar: The Life of a Roman General*. Illustrated by Sam Hadley. New York: The Rosen Publishing Group, Inc., 2005.

What Life Was Like When Rome Ruled the World: The Roman Empire 100 BC – AD 200. Alexandria, VA: Time-Life Books, 1997.

www.historyforkids.org/learn/romans/index.htm
   Provides a general overview of ancient Rome.

172

www.socialstudiesforkids.com/wwww/world/juliuscaesardef.htm
Offers an overview of Caesar's life.

CLEOPATRA

Meltzer, Milton. *Ten Queens: Portraits of Women of Power*. Illustrated by Bethanne Andersen. New York: Dutton Children's Books, 1998.

Sapet, Kerrily. *Cleopatra: Ruler of Egypt*. Greensboro, NC: Morgan Reynolds Publishing, 2007.

Streissguth, Thomas. *Queen Cleopatra*. Minneapolis, MN: Lerner Publications, 2000.

http://school.discoveryeducation.com/schooladventures/cleogame/
Play the "Cleopatra's World" game.

CHRISTOPHER COLUMBUS

Doak, Robin S. *Christopher Columbus: Explorer of the New World*. Minneapolis, MN: Compass Point Books, 2005.

MacDonald, Fiona. *You Wouldn't Want to Sail with Christopher Columbus! Uncharted Waters You'd Rather Not Cross*. Illustrated by David Antram. Danbury, CT: Franklin Watts, 2004.

Pelta, Kathy. *Discovering Christopher Columbus: How History Is Invented*. Minneapolis, MN: Lerner Publications, 1991.

http://video.kids.nationalgeographic.com/video/player/kids/history-kids/
christopher-columbus-kids.html
Watch a video about Columbus and learn how to make a pilgrim ship vegetable platter.

www.columbusnavigation.com
Explores the history, navigation, and landfall of Christopher Columbus.

HENRY VIII

Price, Sean Stewart. *Henry VIII: Royal Beheader*. New York: Franklin Watts, 2009.

www.tudorbritain.org
Find out about Tudor times and play a jousting game.

www.tudorhistory.org/wives
   Learn about Henry's six wives.

ELIZABETH I

Adams, Simon. *Elizabeth I: The Outcast Who Became England's Queen.* Washington DC: National Geographic, 2005.

Stanley, Diane, and Peter Vennema. *Good Queen Bess: The Story of Elizabeth I of England.* New York: HarperCollins, 2001.

Thomas, Jane Resh. *Behind the Mask: The Life of Queen Elizabeth I.* New York: Clarion Books, 1998.

www.elizabethi.org/us
   See what the queen wore, ate, and much more. Visit the Homework Helper feature, too.

www.royal.gov.uk/HistoryoftheMonarchy/KingsandQueensofEngland/TheTudors/ElizabethI.aspx
   The official website of the British monarchy.

POCAHONTAS

Brimner, Larry Dane. *Pocahontas: Bridging Two Worlds.* Tarrytown, NY: Marshall Cavendish Benchmark, 2009.

Fritz, Jean. *The Double Life of Pocahontas.* Puffin Books: New York, 2002.

www.pocahontas.morenus.org
   Compares the Disney movie to the real life of Pocahontas.

GALILEO GALILEI

Doak, Robin S. *Galileo: Astronomer and Physicist.* Minneapolis, MN: Compass Point Books, 2005.

Panchyk, Richard. *Galileo for Kids: His Life and Ideas.* Chicago: Chicago Review Press, 2005.

http://galileo.rice.edu
   A broad look at Galileo's life, work, and family.

http://starchild.gsfc.nasa.gov/docs/StarChild/whos_who_level2/galileo.html
  Helpful links to definitions of some scientific terms.

COOL ARTIFACT—Galileo's middle finger
  http://atlasobscura.com/place/galileos-middle-finger

WOLFGANG AMADEUS MOZART

Stanley, Diane. *Mozart, the Wonder Child: A Puppet Play in Three Acts.* New York: HarperCollins Publishers, 2009.

Weeks, Marcus. *Mozart: The Boy Who Changed the World with His Music.* Washington DC: National Geographic Society, 2007.

www.classicsforkids.com/composers/bio.asp?id=36
  A brief biography of Mozart, plus links to fun games such as "Compose Your Own Music."

www.dsokids.com/listen/ComposerDetail.aspx?composerID=15
  Play three samples of Mozart's music by clicking on the song's play button at the top of the page.

MARIE ANTOINETTE

Bingham, Jane. *Marie Antoinette.* Chicago: Raintree, 2009.

http://en.chateauversailles.fr
  The official site of the Palace of Versailles allows readers to explore the palace Marie Antoinette called home.

www.pbs.org/marieantoinette/index.html
  Offers a timeline, a look into her life as a royal, information on the French Revolution, and a fact-or-fiction quiz.

GEORGE WASHINGTON

Dolan, Edward F. *George Washington.* Tarrytown, NY: Marshall Cavendish Benchmark, 2008.

Harness, Cheryl. *George Washington.* Washington DC: National Geographic Children's Books, 2006.

175

Hort, Lenny. *George Washington.* New York: DK Publishing, 2005.

www.doctorzebra.com/prez/g01.htm
    Detailed medical history about Washington's failing health.

www.georgewashington.si.edu
    Games and a chronology of Washington's life.

COOL ARTIFACT—George Washington's teeth
    www.history.org/foundation/journal/summer05/george_side.cfm

NAPOLEON BONAPARTE

Burleigh, Robert. *Napoleon: The Story of the Little Corporal.* New York: Abrams Books for
    Young Readers and the American Federation of Arts, 2007.

Henderson, Harry. *The Age of Napoleon.* San Diego: Lucent Books, 1999.

www.napoleonguide.com
    Everything Napoleon!

www.napoleon.org/en/kids
    Games, animated timelines, and interactive maps about Napoleon and his times.

COOL ARTIFACT—Napoleon's death mask
    www.liverpoolmuseums.org.uk/nof/top/deathmask.html

LUDWIG VAN BEETHOVEN

January, Brendan. *Ludwig van Beethoven: Musical Genius.* New York: Franklin Watts,
    2004.

Krull, Kathleen. *Lives of the Musicians: Good Times, Bad Times (and What the Neighbors
    Thought).* Illustrated by Kathryn Hewitt. New York: Harcourt, 2002.

Martin, Russell, and Lydia Nibley. *The Mysteries of Beethoven's Hair.* Watertown, MA:
    Charlesbridge, 2009.

www.beethoven-haus-bonn.de/hallo-beethoven/fullscr_e.html
    Explore Beethoven's world.

www.beethovenshair.ca/flash.html
    Follow the journey of Beethoven's hair.

COOL ARTIFACT—Beethoven's death mask
http://socyberty.com/history/death-masks-of-the-famous

EDGAR ALLAN POE

LeVert, Suzanne. *Edgar Allan Poe.* New York: Chelsea House, 1992.

Meltzer, Milton. *Edgar Allan Poe: A Biography.* Minneapolis, MN: Twenty-First Century Books, 2003.

Poe, Edgar Allan. *Edgar Allan Poe's Tales of Mystery and Madness.* Illustrated by Gris Grimly. New York: Atheneum Books for Young Readers, 2004.

http://knowingpoe.thinkport.org
Visit one of the towns Poe lived in and learn about him as a writer and a person.

CHARLES DICKENS

Blishen, Edward. *Stand Up, Mr. Dickens: A Dickens Anthology.* Illustrated by Jill Bennett. Boston: Houghton Mifflin, 1996.

Caravantes, Peggy. *The Best of Times: The Story of Charles Dickens.* Greensboro, NC: Morgan Reynolds Publishing, 2005.

Stanley, Diane, and Peter Vennema. *Charles Dickens: The Man Who Had Great Expectations.* New York: Morrow Junior Books, 1993.

www.bbc.co.uk/drama/bleakhouse/animation.shtml
Funny animated biography of Dickens's life.

www.biography.com/articles/Charles-Dickens-192833
Simple biography of Dickens with links to clips from *Biography* shows about his life.

JAMES A. GARFIELD

Kingsbury, Robert. *The Assassination of James A. Garfield.* New York: The Rosen Publishing Group, Inc., 2002.

Lillegard, Dee. *James A. Garfield: Twentieth President of the United States.* Chicago: Children's Press, 1987.

177

www.doctorzebra.com/prez/g20.htm
Detailed medical health of Garfield and all that led to his death.

www.whitehouse.gov/about/presidents/jamesgarfield
The official White House Garfield biography.

CHARLES DARWIN

Evans, J. Edward. *Charles Darwin: Revolutionary Biologist*. Minneapolis, MN: Lerner Publications, 1993.

Nardo, Don. *The Origin of Species: Darwin's Theory of Evolution*. San Diego: Lucent Books, 2001.

Senker, Cath. *Charles Darwin*. Austin, TX: Raintree Steck-Vaughn, 2002.

www.aboutdarwin.com/darwin/darwin_01.html
This well-designed site is filled with interesting information, including a fascinating section that shows the odd daily schedule Darwin kept.

MARIE CURIE

Cobb, Vicki. *Marie Curie*. New York: DK Publishing, 2008.

Krull, Kathleen. *Marie Curie*. New York: Viking, 2007.

Yannuzzi, Della A. *New Elements: The Story of Marie Curie*. Greensboro, NC: Morgan Reynolds Publishing, 2006.

www.biography.com/articles/Marie-Curie-9263538
Basic biography of the groundbreaking scientist.

ALBERT EINSTEIN

Calaprice, Alice. *Dear Professor Einstein: Albert Einstein's Letters To and From Children*. Amherst, NY: Prometheus Books, 2002.

Delano, Marfé Ferguson. *Genius: A Photobiography of Albert Einstein*. Washington DC: National Geographic Society, 2005.

Krull, Kathleen. *Albert Einstein*. Illustrated by Boris Kulikov. Giants of Science series. New York: Viking, 2009.

Lassieur, Allison. *Albert Einstein: Genius of the Twentieth Century*. New York: Franklin Watts, 2005.

Yeatts, Tabatha. *Albert Einstein: The Miracle Mind*. New York: Sterling, 2007.

www.einstein-website.de/contentskids.html
Easy-to-read biography of Einstein, including a section about Einstein's grades in school. Includes quotes from Einstein's letters to children.

www.pbs.org/wgbh/nova/einstein
Companion to a PBS show; provides in-depth exploration of everything Einstein.

COOL ARTIFACT—Einstein's brain
http://en.wikipedia.org/wiki/Albert_Einstein's_brain

FIND A GRAVE

www.findagrave.com
This wonderful website shows where each individual is buried and also gives a little biographical information. It has great pictures, and readers can leave virtual flowers at the site for the famous faces.

INDEX

INDEX